smoothies, juices & cocktails

THIRST-QUENCHING
RECIPES FOR ALL OCCASIONS

LINDA DOESER &

CHRISTINE AMBRIDGE

This is a Parragon Book
This edition published in 2005

Parragon
Queen Street House
4 Queen Street
Bath BA1 1HE, UK

Created and produced for Parragon by The Bridgewater Book Company Ltd.
Cover by Talking Design

ISBN: 1-40545-841-0

Printed in China

NOTE

*This book uses metric and imperial measurements. Follow the same units of
measurement throughout; do not mix metric and imperial. All spoon measurements
are level: teaspoons are assumed to be 5 ml and tablespoons are assumed to be 15 ml.
Unless otherwise stated, milk is assumed to be full fat, eggs and individual vegetables
such as potatoes are medium, and pepper is freshly ground black pepper.*

*Recipes using raw or very lightly cooked eggs should be avoided by infants, the elderly,
pregnant women, convalescents and anyone suffering from an illness. Pregnant and breastfeeding
women are advised to avoid eating peanuts and peanut products.*

Contents

Introduction 4

Cocktails **6**

Classic Cocktails 12

Contemporary Cocktails 68

Non-alcoholic Cocktails 86

Smoothies & Juices **98**

Fruits 104

Vegetables, Herbs
&t Spices 156

Sweets & Coffees 176

Drinks List 192

Introduction

Nowadays, supermarkets are crammed with bottles, cartons and cans containing hundreds of different drinks, from fruit juice to flavoured yogurts and even ready-mixed cocktails.

Yet, somehow, they never quite live up to their labels and our expectations – they're too sweet, they lack 'bite' or they taste like liquid bubble gum. There's a simple answer – get creative in the

kitchen, and you're holding the key in your hands with this book. Whether you want an energizing booster to start the day, a refreshing cooler in the mid-afternoon, a sophisticated cocktail to set the tone for the evening or a nightcap to help you wind down, you will find the perfect recipe in the following pages.

This book is divided into two main sections. The first part is packed with recipes for classic and contemporary cocktails and even includes a chapter of 'mocktails' – non-alcoholic mixed

drinks. Don't worry if you don't know your Piña Colada from your White Lady; there is helpful advice on what is stirred and what is shaken and how to do it.

The second section provides a cornucopia of recipes for smoothies and juices based on fresh fruit, vegetables, herbs and spices, and coffee and chocolate to set the taste buds singing. A guide to techniques and equipment, much of which you will already have in your kitchen, guarantees success, whether you crave a healthy Banana & Apple Booster or a Rich Chocolate Shake.

Cool in every sense, these drinks are just asking to be shared with friends and family. Cocktails are back in style and today's cocktail party has a new approach that matches the informality of modern life. You can, of course, still wear 'a little black dress' and sip delicately at a Martini, but equally, you can push the boat out with a Full Monty and wear... whatever you like. Coolers and iced teas

are the perfect choices for summer brunches and picnics, while a night in with the girls experimenting with a selection of smoothies is not just fun, but will make you feel virtuously healthy. You could even serve one of the savoury vegetable smoothies as an unusual appetizer to an alfresco meal, or end a summer supper with a refreshing glass of iced coffee.

While cocktails are colourful, festive and delicious, not everyone wants alcoholic drinks, even at a party. It's often difficult to find non-alcoholic drinks to suit adults and they usually end up with boring bottled fruit juice and unexciting mineral water. Both the chapter on non-alcoholic cocktails and most of the second section of this book provide the answer to this dilemma – drinks with a sophisticated edge and adult appeal. Drivers may have to resist the temptation of a Singapore Sling or Bloody Mary, but they will be grateful if you offer them glasses of Grapefruit Cooler or Red Pepper Reactor.

There are great recipes for the kids, too, from irresistible milkshakes to old-fashioned favourites such as lemonade. Freshly made, no artificial flavourings or colourings and, in many instances, much more economical than commercial soft drinks, they're also packed full of vitamins. What parent could ask for more? Of course, the kids just love the flavours and the fun.

None of these drinks is difficult to make and most are virtually instant – all you need is a good stock of ingredients. So get shaking and stirring, juicing and whizzing for the perfect cool drink to suit every occasion.

Cocktails

Precisely where the word 'cocktail' came from is uncertain. A popular piece of folklore describes how a Mexican princess called Xoctl offered a mixed drink to an American visitor to her father's court, who confused her name with that of the drink itself. Other suggestions are based on the fact that non-thoroughbred horses in 18th and 19th century America were referred to as being

'cock-tailed', because their tails looked like those of cockerels. Some say that these horses' docked tails also resembled the spoon used for mixing drinks, leading to imbibing racegoers using the term for the drinks as well; others say that the term for these mixed-blood horses seemed appropriate for a drink made up of so many

different substances. There are many other flights of fancy, but modern etymologists mostly agree that the word derives from *coquetel*, a French, wine-based drink.

Whatever the origins of the word cocktail, mixed drinks have existed since ancient times and the first recognizable cocktail dates from about the 16th century. Indeed, many

classics have been around for much longer than most people think. The bourbon-based Old Fashioned, for example, first appeared at the end of the 18th century. We know that the word cocktail was already in use in 1809 in the United States and, thirty-five years later, when Charles Dickens described Major Pawkins as able to drink 'more rum-toddy, mint-julep, gin-sling and cock-tail than any private gentleman of his acquaintance', it had reached Britain, too.

Popular among the style-conscious and wealthy in the United States, cocktails were served before dinner in the most exclusive houses and hotels until World War I made them unfashionable. They have gone in and out of vogue ever since.

Following the war, young people, disillusioned by the older generation and

desperately seeking new experiences, pleasures, stimuli and styles, developed a taste for a new range of cocktails. Ironically, Prohibition in the United States in the 1920s spurred on their development. Illegally produced liquor frequently tasted poisonous – and sometimes was – so the clubs and speakeasies needed to disguise the flavour with fruit juices and mixers. No doubt, the naughtiness of drinking alcoholic cocktails also added to their appeal to the 'bright young things' of the time. The craze quickly crossed the Atlantic and the best hotels in London, Paris and Monte Carlo, where the quality of gin and whisky was more consistent, soon boasted their own cocktail bars.

World War II brought an end to such revelry and, although drunk occasionally, cocktails remained out of style for decades until an exuberant renaissance in the 1980s. This resulted in another new generation of recipes, often featuring white rum and vodka, as well as tequila, which was just becoming known outside its native Mexico. Inevitably, the pendulum swung again, and cocktails fell from favour until recently. Now, once more, the cocktail shaker is essential equipment in every fashionable city bar.

Equipment

Classic cocktails are either shaken or stirred. A shaker is an essential. It consists of a container with an inner, perforated lid and an outer lid. Both lids are secured while the mixture is shaken, together with cracked ice, and then the cocktail is strained through the perforated lid into a glass.

A mixing glass is a medium-sized jug for preparing stirred cocktails. Uncoloured glass is best, so you can see what you are doing.

A long-handled bar spoon is perfect for stirring and a small strainer prevents the ice cubes – used during mixing – finding their way into the cocktail glass. Some modern cocktails, and any cocktail that is made by shaking, can be made in a blender or food processor, so if you have one, by all means make use of it.

Measuring cups and spoons are essential for getting the proportions right – guessing does not work. A corkscrew, bottle-opener and sharp knife are also crucial.

You can serve cocktails in any glasses you like. Small, V-shaped, stemmed glasses may be worth buying, but it is not essential to have a full range of all the different glasses. Tumblers, small tumblers and wine glasses cover most contingencies. As part of their appeal is visual, cocktails are best served in clear, uncut glasses. Chill the glasses to ensure cocktails are cold.

Ingredients

You can stock your bar over a period of time with the basics – it is not necessary to buy everything at once. A good all-round selection of alcoholic drinks would include whisky, possibly Scotch and bourbon, brandy, gin, light and dark rum, triple sec, sweet and dry vermouth, vodka and tequila. You could also include Pernod, beer and wine. Keep champagne cocktails for special occasions.

Standard mixers include soda water, sparkling mineral water, cola, ginger ale and tonic water. Freshly squeezed fruit juice is best, but when buying juice in a bottle or carton avoid any with added sugar or extra 'padding'. Cranberry juice, for example, may be bulked with grape juice. Commercial brands of grapefruit, orange, cranberry, tomato juice and lime cordial are also useful.

A good supply of fresh lemons, limes and oranges is essential. Fresh fruit is best, but if you use canned, buy it in natural juice (not syrup) and drain well. Other useful ingredients include Angostura bitters, Worcestershire sauce and maraschino cherries. Finally, you can never have too much ice.

Techniques

Store ice in the freezer before using. To crack ice, put ice cubes into a strong polythene bag and hit it against an outside wall, or put the ice between clean cloths on a sturdy surface and crush with a wooden mallet. Cracked ice is used in both shaken and stirred cocktails. To crush ice, crack it as before but break it into much smaller pieces. Use crushed ice in cocktails prepared in a blender.

Glasses can be frosted with sugar (or salt for Margaritas or Salty Dogs). Rub the rim with a wedge of lemon or lime, then dip it into a saucer of caster sugar or fine salt until it is evenly coated.

To make sugar syrup, put 4 tablespoons each of water and caster sugar into a saucepan. Stir over a low heat until the sugar has dissolved. Bring to the boil, then boil, without stirring, for 1–2 minutes. Cool, then refrigerate in a covered container for up to 2 weeks.

To make a shaken cocktail, put cracked ice into a shaker and pour over the other ingredients. Secure the lids and shake vigorously for 20 seconds, or until a frost forms on the outside of the shaker. Strain into a glass and serve at once. To make a stirred cocktail, use fresh cracked ice and pour over the ingredients immediately. Using a long-handled spoon, stir vigorously, without splashing, for 20 seconds, then strain into a glass and serve at once.

Classic
Cocktails

Classic Cocktail

This cannot lay claim to being the first or even the only classic, but it has all the characteristic hallmarks of sophistication associated with cocktails.

serves 1

lemon wedge

1 tsp caster sugar

4–6 cracked ice cubes

2 measures brandy

½ measure clear Curaçao

½ measure maraschino

½ measure lemon juice

halved lemon slice, to decorate

❶ Rub the rim of a chilled cocktail glass with the lemon wedge, then dip in the sugar to frost.

❷ Put the cracked ice cubes into a cocktail shaker. Pour the brandy, Curaçao, maraschino and lemon juice over the ice and shake vigorously until a frost forms.

❸ Strain into the frosted glass and decorate with the halved lemon slice speared on a cocktail stick.

Variations

A number of cocktails are the quintessential classics of their type and named simply after the main ingredient.

Champagne Cocktail: place a sugar cube in the bottom of a chilled champagne flute and dash with Angostura bitters to douse it. Fill the glass with chilled champagne and decorate with a lemon peel twist.

Tequila Cocktail: put 4–6 cracked ice cubes into a cocktail shaker. Dash Angostura bitters over the ice and pour in 3 measures golden tequila, 1 measure lime juice and ½ measure grenadine. Shake vigorously until a frost forms, then strain into a chilled cocktail glass.

Brandy Cocktail: put 4–6 cracked ice cubes into a cocktail shaker. Dash Angostura bitters over the ice and pour in 2 measures brandy and ½ teaspoon sugar syrup (see page 11). Shake vigorously until a frost forms, then strain into a chilled cocktail glass and decorate with a lemon peel twist.

Bartender's Tip

Maraschino is a sweet Italian liqueur made from cherries. It is usually white, but may also be coloured red. The white version is better for most cocktails, because it does not affect the appearance of the finished drink.

Sidecar

Cointreau is the best-known brand of the orange-flavoured liqueur known generically as triple sec. It is drier and stronger than Curaçao and is always colourless.

serves 1

4–6 cracked ice cubes

2 measures brandy

1 measure triple sec

1 measure lemon juice

orange peel twist, to decorate

❶ Put the cracked ice cubes into a cocktail shaker. Pour the brandy, triple sec and lemon juice over the ice and shake vigorously until a frost forms.

❷ Strain into a chilled glass and decorate with the orange peel twist.

Variations

Champagne Sidecar: make a Sidecar, but strain it into a chilled champagne flute and then top it up with chilled champagne.

Chelsea Sidecar: put 4–6 cracked ice cubes into a cocktail shaker. Pour 2 measures gin, 1 measure triple sec and 1 measure lemon juice over the ice. Shake vigorously until a frost forms, then strain into a chilled cocktail glass. Decorate with a lemon peel twist.

Boston Sidecar: put 4–6 cracked ice cubes into a cocktail shaker. Pour 1½ measures white rum, ½ measure brandy, ½ measure triple sec and ½ measure lemon juice over the ice and shake vigorously until a frost forms. Strain into a chilled cocktail glass and decorate with an orange peel twist.

Polish Sidecar: put 4–6 cracked ice cubes into a cocktail shaker. Pour 2 measures gin, 1 measure blackberry brandy and 1 measure lemon juice over the ice. Shake vigorously until a frost forms, then strain into a chilled cocktail glass. Decorate with a fresh blackberry.

Did you know?

You can buy 'ice cubes' made from soapstone. Place them in the freezer to chill and use as you would ice cubes. They will not dilute your cocktails and will last forever.

Stinger

Aptly named, this is a refreshing, clean-tasting cocktail to tantalize the taste buds and make you sit up and take notice. However, bear in mind that it packs a punch; if you have too many, you are likely to keel over.

serves 1

4–6 cracked ice cubes
2 measures brandy
1 measure white crème de menthe

❶ Put the cracked ice cubes into a cocktail shaker. Pour the brandy and crème de menthe over the ice. Shake vigorously until a frost forms.
❷ Strain into a small, chilled highball glass.

Variations

Amaretto Stinger: put 4–6 cracked ice cubes into a cocktail shaker. Pour 2 measures Amaretto and 1 measure white crème de menthe over the ice. Shake vigorously until a frost forms, then strain into a chilled cocktail glass.

Chocolate Stinger: put 4–6 cracked ice cubes into a cocktail shaker. Pour 1 measure dark crème de cacao and 1 measure white crème de menthe over the ice. Shake vigorously until a frost forms. Strain into a chilled cocktail glass.

Irish Stinger: put 4–6 cracked ice cubes into a cocktail shaker. Pour 1 measure Bailey's Irish Cream and 1 measure white crème de menthe over the ice. Shake vigorously until a frost forms, then strain into a chilled shot glass.

Did you know?

Bailey's Irish Cream is the world's top-selling liqueur and accounts for 1 per cent of Eire's export revenue.

American Rose

'A rose by any other name...' – this Oscar-winning cocktail has, rightly, inspired roses across the world. It is truly a thing of beauty and a joy forever.

serves 1

4–6 cracked ice cubes
1½ measures brandy
1 tsp grenadine
½ tsp Pernod
½ fresh peach, peeled and mashed
sparkling wine, to top up
fresh peach wedge, to decorate

❶ Put the cracked ice cubes into a cocktail shaker. Pour the brandy, grenadine and Pernod over the ice and add the mashed peach. Shake vigorously until a frost forms.

❷ Strain into a chilled wine goblet and top up with sparkling wine. Stir gently, then decorate with the peach wedge.

Variations

White Rose: put 4–6 cracked ice cubes into a cocktail shaker. Dash lemon juice over the ice and pour in 3 measures gin, 1 measure maraschino and 1 measure orange juice. Shake until a frost forms. Strain into a chilled cocktail glass.

Jack Rose: put 4–6 cracked ice cubes into a cocktail shaker. Add 2 measures Calvados or applejack brandy, ½ measure lime juice and 1 teaspoon grenadine. Shake vigorously until a frost forms, then strain into a chilled cocktail glass.

English Rose: put 4–6 cracked ice cubes into a cocktail shaker. Dash lemon juice over the ice and pour in 2 measures gin, 2 measures dry vermouth and 1 measure apricot brandy. Shake until a frost forms. Strain into a chilled cocktail glass.

Russian Rose: put 4–6 cracked ice cubes into a glass. Dash orange bitters over the ice and pour in 3 measures strawberry-flavoured vodka, ½ measure dry vermouth and ½ measure grenadine. Stir gently and strain into a chilled cocktail glass.

Bermuda Rose: put 4–6 cracked ice cubes into a cocktail shaker. Pour 2 measures gin, 2 teaspoons apricot brandy, 1 tablespoon lime juice and 2 teaspoons grenadine over the ice. Shake vigorously until a frost forms. Fill a chilled tumbler with crushed ice. Strain the cocktail into the glass and top up with sparkling mineral water. Decorate with a lime slice.

Mint Julep

A julep is simply a mixed drink sweetened with syrup and it dates back to
ancient times. The mint julep was probably first made in the United States,
and is now the official drink of the Kentucky Derby.

serves 1

leaves of 1 fresh mint sprig

1 tbsp sugar syrup (see page 11)

6–8 crushed ice cubes

3 measures bourbon

fresh mint sprig, to decorate

❶ Put the mint leaves and sugar syrup
into a small, chilled glass and mash with
a teaspoon. Add crushed ice to fill the
glass, then add the bourbon.

❷ Decorate with the mint sprig.

Variations

Frozen Mint Julep: put 4–6 crushed ice
cubes into a blender or food processor.
Add 2 measures bourbon, 1 measure
lemon juice, 1 measure sugar syrup
(see page 11) and 6 fresh mint leaves.
Process at low speed until slushy. Pour
into a small, chilled tumbler and decorate
with a fresh mint sprig.

Brandy Julep: fill a chilled tumbler with
cracked ice. Add 2 measures brandy,

1 teaspoon sugar syrup (see page 11)
and 4 fresh mint leaves. Stir well to mix
and decorate with a fresh mint sprig and
a lemon slice. Serve with a straw.

Jocose Julep: put 4–6 crushed ice cubes
into a blender or food processor. Pour
3 measures bourbon, 1 measure green
crème de menthe, 1½ measures lime juice
and 1 teaspoon sugar syrup (see page 11)
over the ice. Add 5 fresh mint leaves.
Process until smooth. Fill a chilled
tumbler with cracked ice cubes and pour
in the cocktail. Top up with sparkling
mineral water and stir gently to mix.
Decorate with a fresh mint sprig.

Did you know?

The word 'julep' is derived from
Persian and came to us via Arabic.
It means rosewater.

Whiskey Sour

Sours are short drinks, flavoured with lemon or lime juice. They can be made with almost any spirit, although Whiskey Sour was the original and, for many, is still the favourite.

serves 1

4–6 cracked ice cubes

2 measures American blended whiskey

1 measure lemon juice

1 tsp sugar syrup (see page 11)

To decorate

maraschino cherry

orange slice

❶ Put the cracked ice cubes into a cocktail shaker. Pour the whiskey, lemon juice and sugar syrup over the ice. Shake vigorously until a frost forms.

❷ Strain into a chilled cocktail glass and decorate with the cherry speared on a cocktail stick and an orange slice.

Variations

Bourbon Sour: substitute bourbon for the whiskey and decorate with an orange slice.

Brandy Sour: substitute 2½ measures brandy for the whiskey.

Boston Sour: add 1 egg white to the ingredients and decorate with a maraschino cherry and a lemon slice.

Polynesian Sour: put 4–6 cracked ice cubes into a cocktail shaker. Pour 2 measures white rum, ½ measure lemon juice, ½ measure orange juice and ½ measure guava juice over the ice. Shake vigorously until a frost forms, then pour into a chilled cocktail glass. Decorate with an orange slice.

Fireman's Sour: put 4–6 cracked ice cubes into a cocktail shaker. Pour 2 measures white rum, 1½ measures lime juice, 1 tablespoon grenadine and 1 teaspoon sugar syrup (see page 11) over the ice. Shake until a frost forms. Strain into a cocktail glass and decorate with a maraschino cherry and a lemon slice.

Strega Sour: put 4–6 cracked ice cubes into a cocktail shaker. Pour 2 measures gin, 1 measure Strega and 1 measure lemon juice over the ice. Shake vigorously until a frost forms. Strain into a cocktail glass and decorate with a lemon slice.

Double Standard Sour: put 4–6 cracked ice cubes into a cocktail shaker. Pour 1½ measures American blended whiskey, 1½ measures gin, 1 measure lemon juice, 1 teaspoon grenadine and 1 teaspoon sugar syrup (see page 11) over the ice. Shake vigorously until a frost forms. Strain into a cocktail glass and decorate with a maraschino cherry and an orange slice.

Manhattan

Said to have been invented by Sir Winston Churchill's American mother,
Jennie, the Manhattan is one of many cocktails named after places in New
York. The centre of sophistication in the Jazz Age, the city is, once again,
buzzing with cocktail bars for a new generation.

serves 1

4–6 cracked ice cubes
dash of Angostura bitters
3 measures rye whiskey
1 measure sweet vermouth
maraschino cherry, to decorate

❶ Put the cracked ice cubes into a mixing glass. Dash the Angostura bitters over the ice and pour in the whiskey and vermouth. Stir well to mix.

❷ Strain into a chilled glass and decorate with the maraschino cherry speared on a cocktail stick.

City lights

Harlem Cocktail: put 4–6 cracked ice cubes into a cocktail shaker. Pour 2 measures gin, 1½ measures pineapple juice and 1 teaspoon maraschino over the ice and add 1 tablespoon chopped fresh pineapple. Shake vigorously until a frost forms, then strain into a small, chilled tumbler.

Brooklyn: put 4–6 cracked ice cubes into a mixing glass. Dash Amer Picon and maraschino over the ice and pour in 2 measures rye whiskey and 1 measure dry vermouth. Stir to mix, then strain into a chilled cocktail glass.

Broadway Smile: pour 1 measure chilled triple sec into a small, chilled tumbler. With a steady hand, pour 1 measure chilled crème de cassis on top, without mixing, then pour 1 measure chilled Swedish Punsch on top, again without mixing.

Fifth Avenue: pour 1½ measures chilled dark crème de cacao into a small, chilled, straight-sided glass. With a steady hand, pour 1½ measures chilled apricot brandy on top, without mixing, then pour ¾ measure chilled single cream on top, again without mixing.

Coney Island Baby: put 4–6 cracked ice cubes into a cocktail shaker. Pour 2 measures peppermint schnapps and 1 measure dark crème de cacao over the ice. Shake vigorously until a frost forms. Fill a small, chilled tumbler with cracked ice and strain the cocktail over it. Top up with soda water and stir gently.

Old Fashioned

So ubiquitous is this cocktail that a small, straight-sided tumbler is known as an Old Fashioned glass. It is a perfect illustration of the saying, 'Sometimes the old ones are the best.'

serves 1

sugar cube

dash of Angostura bitters

1 tsp water

2 measures bourbon or rye whiskey

4–6 cracked ice cubes

lemon peel twist, to decorate

❶ Put the sugar cube into a small, chilled Old Fashioned glass. Dash the Angostura bitters over the cube and add the water. Mash with a spoon until the sugar has dissolved.

❷ Pour the bourbon or rye whiskey into the glass and stir. Add the cracked ice cubes. Decorate with the lemon peel twist.

'Not old, but mellow'

Brandy Old Fashioned: put a sugar cube into a small, chilled tumbler. Dash Angostura bitters over the sugar to douse and add a dash of water. Mash with a spoon until the sugar has dissolved, then pour in 3 measures brandy and add 4–6 cracked ice cubes. Stir gently and decorate with a lemon peel twist.

Old Etonian: put 4–6 cracked ice cubes into a mixing glass. Dash crème de noyaux and orange bitters over the ice and pour in 1 measure gin and 1 measure Lillet. Stir to mix, then strain into a chilled cocktail glass. Squeeze over a piece of orange peel.

Old Pal: put 4–6 cracked ice cubes into a cocktail shaker. Pour 2 measures rye whiskey, 1½ measures Campari and 1 measure sweet vermouth over the ice. Shake vigorously until a frost forms, then strain into a chilled cocktail glass.

Old Trout: put 4–6 cracked ice cubes into a cocktail shaker. Pour 1 measure Campari and 2 measures orange juice over the ice. Shake vigorously until a frost forms. Fill a tall glass with ice cubes and strain the cocktail over them. Top up with sparkling mineral water and decorate with an orange slice.

Old Pale: put 4–6 cracked ice cubes into a mixing glass. Pour 2 measures bourbon, 1 measure Campari and 1 measure dry vermouth over the ice. Stir well, then strain into a chilled cocktail glass. Squeeze over a piece of lemon peel.

Martini

For many, this is the ultimate cocktail. It is named after its inventor, Martini de Anna de Toggia, and not the famous brand of vermouth. The original version comprised equal measures of gin and vermouth, now known as a Fifty-fifty, but the proportions vary, up to the Ultra Dry Martini, when the glass is merely rinsed out with vermouth before the gin is poured in.

serves 1

4–6 cracked ice cubes
3 measures gin
1 tsp dry vermouth, or to taste
cocktail olive, to decorate

❶ Put the cracked ice cubes into a mixing glass. Pour the gin and vermouth over the ice and stir well to mix.

❷ Strain into a chilled cocktail glass and decorate with a cocktail olive speared on a cocktail stick.

Variations

Gibson: decorate with 2–3 cocktail onions, instead of an olive.

Vodka Martini: substitute vodka for the gin.

Tequini: put 4–6 cracked ice cubes into a mixing glass. Dash Angostura bitters over the ice and pour in 3 measures white tequila and ½ measure dry vermouth. Stir well to mix, strain into a chilled cocktail glass and decorate with a lemon twist.

Dirty Martini: put 4–6 cracked ice cubes into a cocktail shaker. Pour 3 measures gin, 1 measure dry vermouth and ½ measure brine from a jar of cocktail olives over the ice. Shake vigorously until a frost forms. Strain into a chilled cocktail glass and decorate with a cocktail olive.

Saketini: put 4–6 cracked ice cubes into a cocktail shaker. Pour 3 measures gin and ½ measure sake over the ice. Shake vigorously until a frost forms. Strain into a chilled cocktail glass and decorate with a lemon peel twist.

Did you know?

Not only did James Bond always demand that his Martini should be shaken, not stirred, but his creator, Ian Fleming, also followed this practice.

Salty Dog

This is another cocktail that has changed since its invention. When it first appeared, gin-based cocktails were by far the most popular, but nowadays a Salty Dog is more frequently made with vodka. You can use either spirit, but the cocktails will have different flavours.

serves 1

1 tbsp granulated sugar
1 tbsp coarse salt
lime wedge
6–8 cracked ice cubes
2 measures vodka
grapefruit juice, to top up

❶ Mix the sugar and salt together in a saucer. Rub the rim of a chilled Collins glass with the lime wedge, then dip it in the sugar and salt mixture to frost.

❷ Fill the glass with cracked ice cubes and pour the vodka over them. Top up with grapefruit juice and stir to mix. Serve with a straw.

Variations

Bride's Mother: put 4–6 cracked ice cubes into a cocktail shaker. Pour 1½ measures sloe gin, 1 measure gin, 2½ measures grapefruit juice and ½ measure sugar syrup (see page 11) over the ice. Shake vigorously until a frost forms, then strain into a chilled cocktail glass.

A J: put 4–6 cracked ice cubes into a cocktail shaker. Pour 1½ measures applejack or apple brandy and 1 measure grapefruit juice over the ice. Shake vigorously until a frost forms, then strain into a chilled cocktail glass.

Midnight Sun: put 4–6 cracked ice cubes into a cocktail shaker. Pour 2 measures aquavit, 1 measure grapefruit juice and ¼ teaspoon grenadine over the ice. Shake vigorously until a frost forms, then strain into a chilled cocktail glass. Decorate with an orange slice.

Blinker: put 4–6 cracked ice cubes into a cocktail shaker. Pour 2 measures rye whiskey, 2½ measures grapefruit juice and 1 teaspoon grenadine over the ice. Shake vigorously until a frost forms, then strain into a chilled cocktail glass.

Woodward: put 4–6 cracked ice cubes into a cocktail shaker. Pour 2 measures Scotch whisky, ½ measure dry vermouth and ½ measure grapefruit juice over the ice. Shake vigorously until a frost forms, then strain into a chilled cocktail glass.

White Lady

Simple, elegant, subtle and much more powerful than appearance suggests, this is the perfect cocktail to serve before an alfresco summer dinner.

serves 1

4–6 cracked ice cubes
2 measures gin
1 measure triple sec
1 measure lemon juice

❶ Put the cracked ice cubes into a cocktail shaker. Pour the gin, triple sec and lemon juice over the ice. Shake vigorously until a frost forms.

❷ Strain into a chilled cocktail glass.

Variations

Green Lady: put 4–6 cracked ice cubes into a cocktail shaker. Dash lime juice over the ice and pour in 2 measures gin and 1 measure green Chartreuse. Shake vigorously until a frost forms, then strain into a chilled cocktail glass.

Creole Lady: put 4–6 cracked ice cubes into a mixing glass. Pour 2 measures bourbon, 1½ measures Madeira and 1 teaspoon grenadine over the ice. Stir well to mix, then strain into a chilled cocktail glass. Decorate with maraschino cherries.

Perfect Lady: put 4–6 cracked ice cubes into a cocktail shaker. Pour 2 measures gin, 1 measure peach brandy and 1 measure lemon juice over the ice. Add 1 teaspoon egg white. Shake until a frost forms. Strain into a chilled cocktail glass.

Apricot Lady: put 4–6 cracked ice cubes into a cocktail shaker. Pour 1½ measures white rum, 1 measure apricot brandy, 1 tablespoon lime juice and ½ teaspoon triple sec over the ice and add 1 egg white. Shake vigorously until a frost forms. Half fill a small, chilled tumbler with cracked ice. Strain the cocktail over the ice and decorate with an orange slice.

Blue Lady: put 4–6 cracked ice cubes into a cocktail shaker. Pour 2½ measures blue Curaçao, 1 measure white crème de cacao and 1 measure single cream over the ice. Shake until a frost forms, then strain into a chilled cocktail glass.

My Fair Lady: put 4–6 cracked ice cubes into a cocktail shaker. Dash strawberry liqueur over the ice. Pour in 2 measures gin, 1 measure orange juice and 1 measure lemon juice and add 1 egg white. Shake vigorously until a frost forms. Strain into a chilled cocktail glass.

Shady Lady: put 4–6 cracked ice cubes into a cocktail shaker. Dash lime juice over the ice and pour in 3 measures tequila, 1 measure apple brandy and 1 measure cranberry juice. Shake until a frost forms. Strain into a chilled cocktail glass.

Tom Collins

This cocktail combines gin, lemon juice and soda water to make a cooling long drink. This is a venerable cocktail, but the progenitor of several generations of the Collins family of drinks, scattered across the globe, was the popular John Collins cocktail.

serves 1

5–6 cracked ice cubes
3 measures gin
2 measures lemon juice
½ measure sugar syrup (see page 11)
soda water, to top up
lemon slice, to decorate

❶ Put the cracked ice cubes into a cocktail shaker. Pour the gin, lemon juice and sugar syrup over the ice. Shake vigorously until a frost forms.

❷ Strain into a tall, chilled tumbler and top up with soda water. Decorate with a lemon slice.

Variations

John Collins: substitute Dutch gin or genever for the dry gin.

Mick Collins: substitute Irish whiskey for the gin.

Pierre Collins: substitute brandy for the gin.

Pedro Collins: substitute white rum for the gin.

Colonel Collins: substitute bourbon for the gin.

Mac Collins: substitute Scotch whisky for the gin.

Ivan Collins: substitute vodka for the gin and decorate with an orange slice and a maraschino cherry.

Belle Collins: crush 2 fresh mint sprigs and place in a tall, chilled tumbler. Add 4–6 crushed ice cubes and pour in 2 measures gin, 1 measure lemon juice and 1 teaspoon sugar syrup (see page 11).

Top up with sparkling mineral water, stir gently and decorate with a fresh mint sprig.

Juan Collins: half fill a chilled tumbler with cracked ice and pour in 2 measures white tequila, 1 measure lemon juice and 1 teaspoon sugar syrup (see page 11). Top up with sparkling mineral water and stir gently. Decorate with a maraschino cherry.

Country Cousin Collins: put 4–6 crushed ice cubes into a blender or food processor. Dash orange bitters over the ice and pour in 2 measures apple brandy, 1 measure lemon juice and ½ teaspoon sugar syrup (see page 11). Blend at medium speed for 10 seconds. Pour into a chilled tumbler and top up with sparkling mineral water. Stir gently and decorate with a lemon slice.

Singapore Sling

In the days of the British Empire, the privileged would gather in the relative cool of the evening at exclusive clubs to refresh parched throats and gossip about the day's events. Those days are long gone, but a Singapore Sling is still the ideal thirst-quencher on hot summer evenings.

serves 1

10–12 cracked ice cubes
2 measures gin
1 measure cherry brandy
1 measure lemon juice
1 tsp grenadine
soda water, to top up

To decorate
lime peel strip
maraschino cherries

❶ Put 4–6 cracked ice cubes into a cocktail shaker. Pour the gin, cherry brandy, lemon juice and grenadine over the ice. Shake vigorously until a frost forms.

❷ Half fill a chilled highball glass with cracked ice cubes and strain the cocktail over them. Top up with soda water and decorate with the lime peel strip, and maraschino cherries speared on a cocktail stick.

Variations

Sweet Singapore Sling: put 4–6 cracked ice cubes into a cocktail shaker. Dash lemon juice over the ice and pour in 1 measure gin and 2 measures cherry brandy. Shake vigorously until a frost forms. Half fill a chilled tumbler with cracked ice cubes and strain the cocktail over them. Top up with soda water and decorate with maraschino cherries.

Gin Sling: put 1 teaspoon sugar in a mixing glass. Add 1 measure lemon juice and 1 teaspoon water and stir until the sugar has dissolved. Pour in 2 measures gin and stir to mix. Half fill a small, chilled tumbler with ice and strain the cocktail over it. Decorate with an orange twist.

Whiskey Sling: put 1 teaspoon sugar in a mixing glass. Add 1 measure lemon juice and 1 teaspoon water and stir until the sugar has dissolved. Pour in 2 measures American blended whiskey and stir to mix. Half fill a small, chilled tumbler with ice and strain the cocktail over it. Decorate with an orange twist.

Long Island Iced Tea

Like many other classics, this cocktail dates from the days of the American Prohibition, when it was drunk from tea cups in an unconvincing attempt to fool the FBI that it was a harmless beverage. It started out life as a simple combination of vodka coloured with a dash of cola, but has evolved into a more elaborate, but no less potent, concoction.

serves 1

10–12 cracked ice cubes

2 measures vodka

1 measure gin

1 measure white tequila

1 measure white rum

½ measure white crème de menthe

2 measures lemon juice

1 tsp sugar syrup (see page 11)

cola, to top up

lime or lemon wedge, to decorate

❶ Put 4–6 cracked ice cubes into a cocktail shaker. Pour the vodka, gin, tequila, rum, crème de menthe, lemon juice and sugar syrup over the ice. Shake vigorously until a frost forms.

❷ Half fill a tall, chilled tumbler with cracked ice cubes and strain the cocktail over them. Top up with cola and decorate with the lime or lemon wedge.

Brewing up

Artillery Punch (to serve 30): pour 1 litre/ 1¾ pints bourbon, 1 litre/1¾ pints red wine, 1 litre/1¾ pints strong black tea, 475 ml/ 17 fl oz dark rum, 250 ml/9 fl oz gin, 250 ml/9 fl oz apricot brandy, 4 measures lemon juice, 4 measures lime juice and 4 tablespoons sugar syrup (see page 11) into a large bowl. Chill for 2 hours. To serve, put a large block of ice into a punch bowl. Pour the punch over the ice and decorate with thin slices of lemon and lime.

Did you know?

In 1920, there were about 15,000 bars in New York. Following the introduction of Prohibition in 1920, the number of illegal speakeasies rocketed to some 32,000.

Piña Colada

One of the younger generation of classics, this became popular during the
cocktail revival of the 1980s and has remained so ever since.

serves 1

4–6 crushed ice cubes
2 measures white rum
1 measure dark rum
3 measures pineapple juice
2 measures coconut cream
fresh pineapple wedges, to decorate

❶ Put the crushed ice into a blender or
food processor and add the white rum,
dark rum, pineapple juice and coconut
cream. Blend until smooth.

❷ Pour, without straining, into a tall,
chilled glass and decorate with pineapple
wedges speared on a cocktail stick.

Variations

Lighten Up Piña Colada: put 4–6
cracked ice cubes into a cocktail shaker.
Pour 2 measures white rum, 2 measures
Malibu and 3 measures pineapple juice
over the ice. Shake vigorously until a frost
forms. Half fill a small, chilled tumbler
with cracked ice cubes and strain the
cocktail over them. Decorate with a fresh
pineapple slice.

Amigos Piña Colada (to serve 4): put
10–12 crushed ice cubes into a blender or
food processor and add 250 ml/9 fl oz white
rum, 300 ml/10 fl oz pineapple juice,
5 measures coconut cream, 2 measures
dark rum and 2 measures single cream.
Blend until smooth. Pour, without
straining, into tall, chilled tumblers and
decorate with fresh pineapple wedges
speared on cocktail sticks.

Strawberry Colada: put 4–6 crushed ice
cubes into a blender or food processor
and add 3 measures golden rum,
4 measures pineapple juice, 1 measure
coconut cream and 6 hulled fresh
strawberries. Blend until smooth. Pour,
without straining, into a tall, chilled
tumbler. Decorate with fresh pineapple
wedges and strawberries speared on a
cocktail stick.

Banana Colada: put 4–6 crushed ice
cubes into a blender or food processor
and add 2 measures white rum,
4 measures pineapple juice, 1 measure
Malibu and 1 peeled and sliced banana.
Blend until smooth. Pour, without
straining, into a tall, chilled tumbler and
serve with a straw.

Acapulco

This is one of many cocktails that has changed from its original recipe over the years. To begin with, it was always rum-based and did not include any fruit juice. Nowadays, it is increasingly made with tequila, because this has become better known outside its native Mexico.

serves 1

10–12 cracked ice cubes
2 measures white rum
½ measure triple sec
½ measure lime juice
1 tsp sugar syrup (see page 11)
1 egg white
fresh mint sprig, to decorate

❶ Put 4–6 cracked ice cubes into a cocktail shaker. Pour the rum, triple sec, lime juice and sugar syrup over the ice and add the egg white. Shake vigorously until a frost forms.

❷ Half fill a chilled highball glass with cracked ice cubes and strain the cocktail over them. Decorate with the mint sprig.

Variations

Acapulco Gold: put 4–6 cracked ice cubes into a cocktail shaker. Pour 1 measure golden tequila, 1 measure golden rum, 2 measures pineapple juice, 1 measure coconut cream and 1 measure grapefruit juice over the ice. Shake vigorously until a frost forms. Half fill a small, chilled tumbler with cracked ice cubes and strain the cocktail over them.

Acapulco Clam Digger: put 4–6 cracked ice cubes into a tall tumbler. Dash Tabasco sauce, Worcestershire sauce and lemon juice over the ice and pour in 1½ measures white tequila, 3 measures tomato juice and 3 measures clam juice. Add 2 teaspoons horseradish sauce. Stir well to mix, decorate with a lime slice and serve with a straw.

Did you know?

Rum owes its origin to Christopher Columbus, who is said to have planted the first sugar cane in the islands of the Caribbean.

Daiquiri

Daiquiri is a town in Cuba, where this drink was said to have been invented in the early part of the 20th century. A businessman had run out of imported gin and so had to make do with the local drink – rum – which, at that time, was of unreliable quality. To ensure that his guests would find it palatable, he mixed it with other ingredients. This classic has since given rise to almost innumerable variations.

serves 1

4–6 cracked ice cubes
2 measures white rum
¾ measure lime juice
½ tsp sugar syrup (see page 11)

❶ Put the cracked ice cubes into a cocktail shaker. Pour the rum, lime juice and sugar syrup over the ice. Shake vigorously until a frost forms.
❷ Strain into a chilled cocktail glass.

Variations

Derby Daiquiri: put 4–6 crushed ice cubes into a blender or food processor and add 2 measures white rum, 1 measure orange juice, ½ measure triple sec and ½ measure lime juice. Blend until smooth. Pour, without straining, into a chilled cocktail glass.

Banana Daiquiri: put 4–6 crushed ice cubes into a blender or food processor and add 2 measures white rum, ½ measure triple sec, ½ measure lime juice, ½ measure single cream, 1 teaspoon sugar syrup (see page 11) and ¼ peeled and sliced banana. Blend until smooth. Pour the mixture, without straining, into a chilled goblet and decorate with a lime slice.

Peach Daiquiri: put 4–6 crushed ice cubes into a blender or food processor and add 2 measures white rum, 1 measure lime juice, ½ teaspoon sugar syrup (see page 11) and ½ peeled and chopped peach. Blend until smooth. Pour, without straining, into a chilled goblet.

Passionate Daiquiri: put 4–6 cracked ice cubes into a cocktail shaker. Pour 2 measures white rum, 1 measure lime juice and ½ measure passion fruit syrup over the ice. Shake vigorously until a frost forms. Strain into a chilled cocktail glass and decorate with a maraschino cherry.

Bartender's Tip
For other Daiquiri variations, see page 70.

Cuba Libre

The 1960s and 1970s saw the meteoric rise in popularity of this simple long drink, perhaps because of highly successful marketing by Bacardi brand rum – the original white Cuban rum (now produced in the Bahamas) – and Coca-Cola, but more likely because rum and cola seem to be natural companions.

serves 1

4–6 cracked ice cubes
2 measures white rum
cola, to top up
lime wedge, to decorate

❶ Half fill a highball glass with cracked ice cubes. Pour the rum over the ice and top up with cola.

❷ Stir gently to mix and decorate with a lime wedge.

Other Cuban classics

Bacardi Cocktail: put 4–6 cracked ice cubes into a cocktail shaker. Pour 2 measures Bacardi rum, 1 measure grenadine and 1 measure fresh lime juice over the ice. Shake vigorously until a frost forms. Strain into a chilled cocktail glass.

Brandy Cuban: half fill a chilled tumbler with cracked ice cubes. Pour 1½ measures brandy and ½ measure lime juice over the ice. Top up with cola and stir gently. Decorate with a lime slice.

Cuban: put 4–6 cracked ice cubes into a cocktail shaker. Pour 2 measures brandy, 1 measure apricot brandy, 1 measure lime juice and 1 teaspoon white rum over the ice. Shake vigorously until a frost forms. Strain into a chilled cocktail glass.

Cuban Special: put 4–6 cracked ice cubes into a cocktail shaker. Pour 2 measures rum, 1 measure lime juice, 1 tablespoon pineapple juice and 1 teaspoon triple sec over the ice. Shake until a frost forms. Strain into a chilled cocktail glass and decorate with a fresh pineapple wedge.

Did you know?

Britain's Royal Navy continued to provide sailors with a daily rum ration until 1969, although, by then, the quantity had been reduced from the original 300 ml/10 fl oz.

Zombie

The individual ingredients of this cocktail, including liqueurs and fruit juices, vary considerably from one recipe to another, but all zombies contain a mixture of white, golden and dark rum in a range of proportions.

serves 1

4–6 crushed ice cubes

2 measures dark rum

2 measures white rum

1 measure golden rum

1 measure triple sec

1 measure lime juice

1 measure orange juice

1 measure pineapple juice

1 measure guava juice

1 tbsp grenadine

1 tbsp orgeat

1 tsp Pernod

To decorate

fresh mint sprig

fresh pineapple wedges

maraschino cherry

❶ Put the crushed ice into a blender or food processor and add the three rums, triple sec, lime juice, orange juice, pineapple juice, guava juice, grenadine, orgeat and Pernod. Blend until smooth.

❷ Pour, without straining, into a tall, chilled Collins glass and decorate with the mint sprig, and pineapple wedges and cherry speared on a cocktail stick.

Variations

Walking Zombie: put 4–6 cracked ice cubes into a cocktail shaker. Pour 1 measure white rum, 1 measure golden rum, 1 measure dark rum, 1 measure apricot brandy, 1 measure lime juice, 1 measure pineapple juice and 1 teaspoon sugar syrup (see page 11) over the ice. Shake vigorously until a frost forms. Half fill a chilled tumbler with cracked ice cubes and strain the cocktail over them. Decorate with orange and lemon slices.
Zombie Prince: put 4–6 cracked ice cubes into a mixing glass. Dash Angostura bitters over the ice, pour in 1 measure white rum, 1 measure golden rum, 1 measure dark rum, ½ measure lemon juice, ½ measure orange juice and ½ measure grapefruit juice and add 1 teaspoon brown sugar. Stir to mix well, then strain into a tall, chilled tumbler.

Bartender's Tip
Orgeat is an almond-flavoured syrup. If you can't find it, you could substitute the same amount of Amaretto, which is more widely available.

Mai Tai

For some reason, this cocktail always inspires elaborate decoration with paper parasols, a selection of fruit and spirals of citrus peel – sometimes so much so that you can be in danger of stabbing your nose on a cocktail stick when you try to drink it. If you want to go completely over the top with decorations – and why not – serving the drink with one or two long, colourful straws might be a good idea.

serves 1

4–6 cracked ice cubes

2 measures white rum

2 measures dark rum

1 measure clear Curaçao

1 measure lime juice

1 tbsp orgeat

1 tbsp grenadine

To decorate

fresh pineapple wedges

maraschino cherry

orchid (optional)

paper parasol (optional)

❶ Put the cracked ice cubes into a cocktail shaker. Pour the white and dark rums, Curaçao, lime juice, orgeat and grenadine over the ice. Shake vigorously until a frost forms.

❷ Strain into a chilled Collins glass and decorate with the pineapple wedges and maraschino cherry speared on a cocktail stick, adding an orchid and paper parasol if desired.

Other decorated cocktails

Generally speaking, you can decorate cocktails in any way you like – or not at all, if you prefer. There are some, however, that are traditionally served in a particular way. The Martini and the Gibson (see page 30), for example, are differentiated only because the former is decorated with a cocktail olive, while the latter is always served with cocktail onions.

Horse's Neck: hang a long spiral of lemon peel over the rim of a tall, chilled tumbler. Fill the glass with cracked ice and pour 2 measures American blended whiskey over the ice. Top up with ginger ale and stir.

Ultimate Beefeater Martini: put 4–6 cracked ice cubes into a mixing glass. Dash dry vermouth over the ice and pour in 1 measure Beefeater gin. Stir well and strain the mixture into a chilled cocktail glass. Decorate with a sliver of fillet steak.

Margarita

The traditional way to drink tequila is to shake a little salt on the back of your hand between the thumb and forefinger and, holding a wedge of lime or lemon, lick the salt, suck the fruit and then down a shot of tequila in one. This cocktail, attributed to Francisco Morales and invented in 1942 in Mexico, is a more civilized version.

serves 1

lime wedge

coarse salt

4–6 cracked ice cubes

3 measures white tequila

1 measure triple sec

2 measures lime juice

halved lime slice, to decorate

❶ Rub the rim of a chilled cocktail glass with the lime wedge and then dip in a saucer of coarse salt to frost.

❷ Put the cracked ice cubes into a cocktail shaker. Pour the tequila, triple sec and lime juice over the ice. Shake vigorously until a frost forms.

❸ Strain into the prepared glass and decorate with the halved lime slice.

Variations

Frozen Margarita: put 6–8 cracked ice cubes into a blender or food processor and add 2 measures white tequila, 1 measure lime juice and ½ measure triple sec. Blend at low speed until slushy. Pour, without straining, into a chilled cocktail glass and decorate with a lime slice.

Blue Margarita: frost the rim of a chilled cocktail glass using a lime wedge and coarse salt (as above). Put 4–6 cracked ice cubes into a cocktail shaker. Pour 2 measures white tequila, 1 measure blue Curaçao, 1½ measures lime juice and 1 tablespoon triple sec over the ice. Shake vigorously until a frost forms. Strain into the prepared glass and decorate with a lime slice.

Margarita Impériale: put 4–6 cracked ice cubes into a cocktail shaker. Dash clear Curaçao over the ice and pour in 1 measure white tequila, 1 measure Mandarine Napoléon and 1 measure lemon juice. Shake vigorously until a frost forms. Strain into a chilled cocktail glass.

Peach Margarita: frost the rim of a chilled cocktail glass using a lime wedge and coarse salt (as above). Put 4–6 cracked ice cubes into a cocktail shaker. Pour 2 measures white tequila, 2 measures lime juice, ½ measure peach liqueur and 1 tablespoon triple sec over the ice. Shake vigorously until a frost forms, then strain into the prepared glass. Decorate with a fresh peach slice.

Tequila Sunrise

This is one cocktail you shouldn't rush when making, otherwise you will spoil the attractive sunrise effect as the grenadine slowly spreads through the orange juice.

serves 1

4–6 cracked ice cubes
2 parts white tequila
orange juice, to top up
1 measure grenadine

❶ Put the cracked ice cubes into a chilled highball glass. Pour the tequila over the ice and top up with the orange juice. Stir well to mix.

❷ Slowly pour in the grenadine and serve with a straw.

Variations

Blinding Sunrise: put 4–6 cracked ice cubes into a cocktail shaker. Pour 1 measure white tequila, 1 measure vodka, 3 measures orange juice and 1 teaspoon triple sec over the ice. Shake vigorously until a frost forms. Half fill a tumbler with cracked ice cubes and strain the cocktail over them. Slowly pour in 1 measure grenadine.

Pacific Sunrise: put 4–6 cracked ice cubes into a cocktail shaker. Dash Angostura bitters over the ice and pour in 1 measure white tequila, 1 measure blue Curaçao and 1 measure lime juice. Shake vigorously until a frost forms, then strain into a chilled cocktail glass.

Mint Sunrise: put 4–6 cracked ice cubes into a chilled tumbler. Pour 1½ measures Scotch whisky, ½ measure brandy and ½ measure clear Curaçao over the ice and stir gently. Decorate with a fresh mint sprig and a lemon slice.

Did you know?

The global popularity of tequila took producers by surprise. The agave plant from which it is made takes 8–10 years to mature: due to this long maturation time, and cultivation problems that subsequently developed, a severe shortage arose by the year 2000, which resulted in rocketing prices and a lucrative trade in 'cactus rustling'.

Bloody Mary

This classic cocktail was invented in 1921 at the legendary Harry's Bar in Paris. There are numerous versions – some much hotter and spicier than others. Ingredients may include horseradish sauce in addition to or instead of Tabasco sauce, more or less tomato juice and lime juice instead of lemon. Sometimes the glass is decorated with a sprig of mint. Whatever the version, all experts agree that it is essential to use the highest-quality ingredients.

serves 1

4–6 cracked ice cubes
dash of Worcestershire sauce
dash of Tabasco sauce
2 measures vodka
6 measures tomato juice
juice of ½ lemon
pinch of celery salt
pinch of cayenne pepper

To decorate
celery stick with leaves
lemon slice

❶ Put the cracked ice cubes into a cocktail shaker. Dash the Worcestershire sauce and Tabasco sauce over the ice and pour in the vodka, tomato juice and lemon juice. Shake vigorously until a frost forms.

❷ Strain into a tall, chilled glass, add a pinch of celery salt and a pinch of cayenne and decorate with a celery stick and a lemon slice.

Variations

Bloody Maria: substitute 2 measures white tequila for the vodka, then add 1 teaspoon horseradish sauce and a pinch of ground coriander. Decorate with a lime wedge.

Cold and Clammy Bloody Mary: substitute 3 measures clam juice for 3 of the measures of tomato juice and decorate with a spring onion curl.

Bullshot: substitute 4 measures chilled beef stock for the tomato juice and season to taste with salt and pepper.

Moscow Mule

This cocktail came into existence through a happy coincidence during the 1930s. An American bar owner had overstocked ginger beer, and a representative of a soft drinks company invented the Moscow Mule to help him out.

serves 1

10–12 cracked ice cubes
2 measures vodka
1 measure lime juice
ginger beer, to top up
lime slice, to decorate

❶ Put 4–6 cracked ice cubes into a cocktail shaker. Pour the vodka and lime juice over the ice. Shake vigorously until a frost forms.

❷ Half fill a chilled highball glass with cracked ice cubes and strain the cocktail over them. Top up with ginger beer. Decorate with a lime slice.

Other stubborn drinks

Delft Donkey: make a Moscow Mule but substitute gin for the vodka.

Mississippi Mule: put 4–6 cracked ice cubes into a cocktail shaker. Pour 2 measures gin, ½ measure crème de cassis and ½ measure lemon juice over the ice. Shake vigorously until a frost forms, then strain into a small, chilled tumbler.

Mule's Hind Leg: put 4–6 cracked ice cubes into a cocktail shaker. Pour ½ measure apricot brandy, ½ measure apple brandy, ½ measure Bénédictine, ½ measure gin and ½ measure maple syrup over the ice. Shake vigorously until a frost forms, then strain into a chilled cocktail glass.

Jamaica Mule: put 4–6 cracked ice cubes into a cocktail shaker. Pour 2 measures white rum, 1 measure dark rum, 1 measure golden rum, 1 measure Falernum and 1 measure lime juice over the ice. Shake vigorously until a frost forms, then strain the mixture into a tall, chilled glass. Top up with ginger beer and decorate with some fresh pineapple wedges and crystallized ginger.

Bartender's Tip

Falernum is a Caribbean syrup used in rum drinks. It is flavoured with lime juice, almonds, ginger and spices.

Screwdriver

Always use freshly squeezed orange juice to make this refreshing cocktail – it is just not the same with bottled juice. This simple, classic cocktail has given rise to numerous and increasingly elaborate variations.

serves 1

6–8 cracked ice cubes
2 measures vodka
orange juice, to top up
orange slice, to decorate

❶ Fill a chilled highball glass with cracked ice cubes. Pour the vodka over the ice and top up with orange juice.

❷ Stir well to mix and decorate with an orange slice.

Variations

Cordless Screwdriver: pour 2 measures chilled vodka into a shot glass. Dip a wedge of orange into caster sugar. Down the vodka in one go and suck the orange.

Creamy Screwdriver: put 4–6 crushed ice cubes into a blender or food processor and add 2 measures vodka, 6 measures orange juice, 1 egg yolk and ½ teaspoon sugar syrup (see page 11). Blend until smooth. Half fill a tall, chilled tumbler with cracked ice cubes and pour the cocktail over them without straining.

Harvey Wallbanger: make a Screwdriver, then float 1 measure Galliano on top by pouring it gently over the back of a teaspoon.

Slow Screw: substitute sloe gin for the vodka.

Bartender's Tip

Galliano is a honey- and vanilla-flavoured liqueur from Italy. It is sold in tall, thin bottles, so bars store it on a top shelf up against the wall to avoid knocking it over.

Did you know?

The Harvey Wallbanger is named after a California surfer who took such prodigious delight in drinking Screwdrivers topped with a Galliano float that he ricocheted from wall to wall on leaving the bar.

Kir

As with the best mustard, crème de cassis production is centred on the French city of Dijon. This cocktail is named in commemoration of a partisan and mayor of the city, Félix Kir.

serves 1

4–6 cracked ice cubes
2 measures crème de cassis
white wine, to top up
lemon peel twist, to decorate

❶ Put the cracked ice cubes into a chilled wine glass. Pour the crème de cassis over the ice.

❷ Top up with chilled white wine and stir well. Decorate with the lemon peel twist.

Wine toppers

Kir Royale: substitute champagne for the white wine.

Osborne (named after Queen Victoria's Isle of Wight residence and apparently a favourite tipple of Her Majesty's): pour 3 measures claret and 1 measure Scotch whisky into a goblet and stir to mix.

Bellini (created at Harry's Bar, Venice, and named after the Renaissance artist): fill a goblet with crushed ice and dash over grenadine. Pour in 1 measure peach juice, then top up with chilled champagne. Decorate with a peeled fresh peach slice.

Bellinitini: put 4–6 cracked ice cubes into a cocktail shaker. Pour in 2 measures vodka, 1 measure peach schnapps and 1 measure peach juice. Shake vigorously until a frost forms, then strain into a chilled goblet. Top up with chilled champagne.

Rikki-Tikki-Tavi: put a sugar cube into a chilled champagne flute and dash Angostura bitters over it until red but still intact. Pour in 1 teaspoon brandy and 1 teaspoon clear Curaçao, then top up with chilled champagne.

Champagne Pick-me-up: put 4–6 cracked ice cubes into a cocktail shaker. Dash grenadine over the ice and then pour in 2 measures brandy, 1 measure orange juice and 1 measure lemon juice. Shake vigorously until a frost forms. Strain the mixture into a wine glass and top up with chilled champagne.

Buck's Fizz

Invented at Buck's Club in London, the original was invariably made with Bollinger champagne and it is true that the better the quality of the champagne, the better the flavour.

serves 1

2 measures chilled champagne

2 measures chilled orange juice

❶ Pour the champagne into a chilled champagne flute, then pour in the orange juice.

Variations

Duck's Fizz: substitute Canard-Duchêne champagne for the Bollinger.

Mimosa: pour the orange juice into the flute and then the champagne. Stir gently. You can use sparkling white wine instead of champagne.

Black Velvet: pour 300 ml/10 fl oz chilled champagne or sparkling wine and 300 ml/10 fl oz chilled stout into a chilled tumbler at the same time. Do not stir.

Soyer au Champagne: put 1 scoop vanilla ice cream into a wine glass and add ¼ teaspoon brandy, ¼ teaspoon triple sec

and ¼ teaspoon maraschino. Stir to mix, then top up with chilled champagne. Stir gently and decorate with a maraschino cherry.

Champagne Cup: pour ½ measure brandy and ½ measure clear Curaçao into a chilled wine glass. Add 1 ice cube and top up with champagne. Decorate with a sprig of fresh mint and an orange slice.

Spritzer: fill a wine glass with cracked ice cubes and pour in 3 measures white wine. Top up with soda water or sparkling mineral water and decorate with a lemon peel twist.

Did you know?

In spite of his ruthless ambition and Prussian earnestness, Otto von Bismarck must have had a more frivolous side to his nature because he is reputed to have created the Black Velvet.

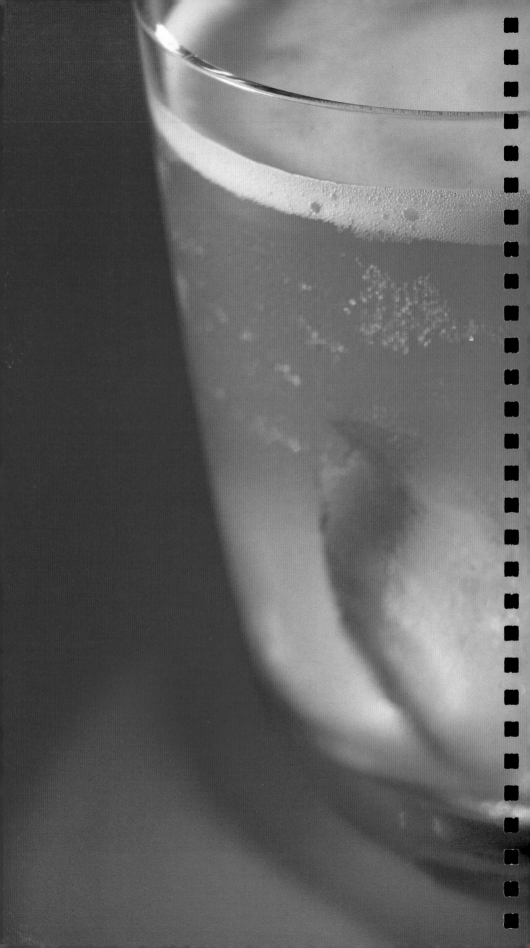

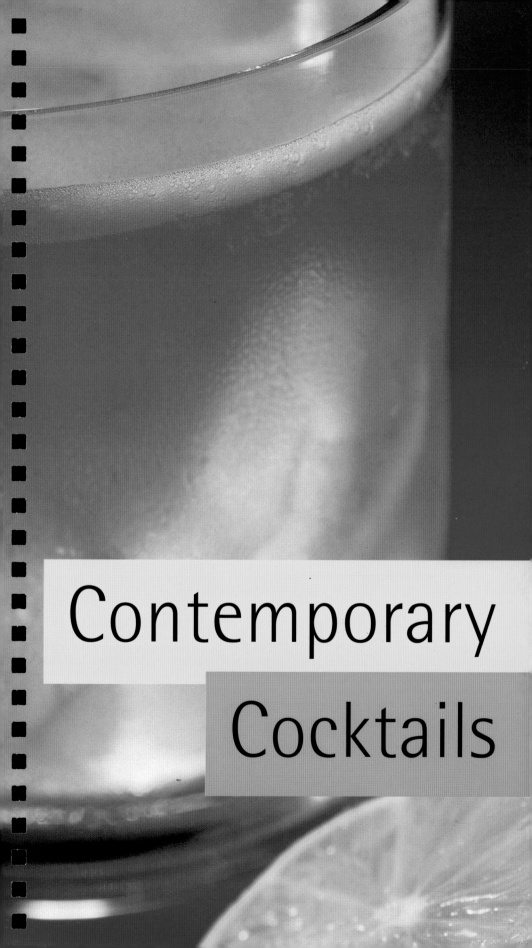

Contemporary Cocktails

Frozen Daiquiri

One of the great classic cocktails, the Daiquiri (see page 46) has moved on. It's not just mixed with fresh fruit or unusual ingredients, it's entered the 21st century with a whole new future, as slushes take on a leading role in fashionable cocktail bars.

serves 1

6 crushed ice cubes

2 measures white rum

1 measure lime juice

1 tsp sugar syrup (see page 11)

lime slice, to decorate

❶ Put the crushed ice into a blender or food processor and add the rum, lime juice and sugar syrup. Blend until slushy.

❷ Pour into a chilled champagne flute and decorate with the lime slice.

Variations

Frozen Pineapple Daiquiri: put 6 crushed ice cubes into a blender or food processor and add 2 measures white rum, 1 measure lime juice, ½ teaspoon pineapple syrup and 55 g/2 oz finely chopped fresh pineapple. Blend until slushy. Pour into a chilled cocktail glass. Decorate with fresh pineapple wedges.

Frozen Mint Daiquiri: put 6 crushed ice cubes into a blender or food processor and add 2 measures white rum, ½ measure lime juice, 1 teaspoon sugar syrup (see page 11) and 6 fresh mint leaves. Blend until slushy. Pour into a chilled cocktail glass.

Frozen Strawberry Daiquiri: put 6 crushed ice cubes into a blender or food processor and add 2 measures white rum, 1 measure lime juice, 1 teaspoon sugar syrup (see page 11) and 6 fresh or frozen strawberries. Blend until slushy. Pour into a cocktail glass. Decorate with a fresh strawberry.

Frozen Peach Daiquiri: put 6 crushed ice cubes into a blender or food processor. Add 2 measures white rum, 1 measure lime juice, 1 teaspoon sugar syrup (see page 11) and ½ peeled and chopped peach. Blend until slushy. Pour into a chilled cocktail glass. Decorate with a fresh peach slice.

Tequila Slammer

Slammers, also known as shooters, are currently very fashionable. The idea is that you pour the different ingredients directly into the glass, normally without stirring (some slammers form colourful layers). Cover the top of the glass with one hand to prevent spillage, then slam the glass on the bar or a table to mix and drink the cocktail down in one. It is essential to use a strong glass that is unlikely to break under such treatment.

serves 1

1 measure white tequila
1 measure lemon juice
chilled sparkling wine, to top up

❶ Put the tequila and lemon juice into a chilled glass and stir to mix. Top up with sparkling wine.

❷ Cover the glass with your hand and slam.

'Those little shooters, how I love to drink them down...'

Alabama Slammer: put 4–6 cracked ice cubes into a mixing glass. Pour 1 measure Southern Comfort, 1 measure Amaretto and ½ measure sloe gin over the ice and stir to mix. Strain into a shot glass and add ½ teaspoon lemon juice. Cover and slam.

B52: pour 1 measure chilled dark crème de cacao into a shot glass. With a steady hand, gently pour in 1 measure chilled Bailey's Irish Cream to make a second layer, then gently pour in 1 measure chilled Grand Marnier. Cover and slam.

B52 (second version): pour 1 measure chilled Kahlúa into a shot glass. With a steady hand, gently pour in 1 measure chilled Bailey's Irish Cream to make a second layer, then gently pour in 1 measure chilled Grand Marnier. Cover and slam.

Banana Slip: pour 1 measure chilled crème de banane into a shot glass. With a steady hand, gently pour in 1 measure chilled Bailey's Irish Cream to make a second layer. Cover and slam.

Wild Night Out

Tequila has a reputation for being an extraordinarily potent spirit, but most commercially exported brands are the same standard strength as other spirits, such as gin or whisky. 'Home-grown' tequila or its close relative, *mescal*, may be another matter.

serves 1

10–12 cracked ice cubes
3 measures white tequila
2 measures cranberry juice
1 measure lime juice
soda water, to top up

❶ Put 4–6 cracked ice cubes into a cocktail shaker. Pour the tequila, cranberry juice and lime juice over the ice. Shake vigorously until a frost forms.
❷ Half fill a chilled highball glass with cracked ice cubes and strain the cocktail over them. Add soda water to taste.

The wild bunch

Buttafuoco: put 4–6 cracked ice cubes into a cocktail shaker. Pour 2 measures white tequila, ½ measure Galliano, ½ measure cherry brandy and ½ measure lemon juice over the ice. Shake vigorously until a frost forms. Half fill a tumbler with cracked ice cubes and strain the cocktail over them. Top up with soda water and decorate with a maraschino cherry.

Magna Carta: rub the rim of a wine glass with a wedge of lime, then dip in caster sugar to frost. Put 4–6 cracked ice cubes into a mixing glass. Pour 2 measures white tequila and 1 measure triple sec over the ice and stir well to mix. Strain into the prepared glass and top up with chilled sparkling wine.

Tequila Fizz: put 4–6 cracked ice cubes into a cocktail shaker. Pour 3 measures white tequila, 1 measure grenadine and 1 measure lime juice over the ice and add 1 egg white. Shake vigorously until a frost forms. Half fill a chilled tumbler with cracked ice cubes and strain the cocktail over them. Top up with ginger ale.

Changuirongo: half fill a tall, chilled tumbler with cracked ice cubes. Pour 2 measures white tequila over the ice and top up with ginger ale. Stir gently and decorate with a lime slice.

Carolina

White tequila is most commonly used for mixing cocktails, but some require the more mellow flavour of the amber-coloured, aged tequilas, which are known as golden tequila or *añejo*.

serves 1

4–6 cracked ice cubes
3 measures golden tequila
1 tsp grenadine
1 tsp vanilla essence
1 measure single cream
1 egg white

To decorate
ground cinnamon
maraschino cherry

❶ Put the cracked ice cubes into a cocktail shaker. Pour the tequila, grenadine, vanilla essence and cream over the ice and add the egg white. Shake vigorously until a frost forms.
❷ Strain into a chilled cocktail glass. Sprinkle with cinnamon and decorate with a maraschino cherry speared on a cocktail stick.

The golden touch

Grapeshot: put 4–6 cracked ice cubes into a cocktail shaker. Pour 2 measures golden tequila, 1 measure clear Curaçao and 1½ measures white grape juice over the ice and shake vigorously until a frost forms. Strain into a chilled cocktail glass.
Montezuma: put 4–6 crushed ice cubes into a blender or food processor and add 2 measures golden tequila, 1 measure Madeira and 1 egg yolk. Blend until smooth. Pour into a chilled cocktail glass.
Chapala: put 4–6 cracked ice cubes into a cocktail shaker. Pour 2 measures golden tequila, 2 measures orange juice, 1 measure lime juice, ½ measure triple sec and ½ measure grenadine over the ice. Shake vigorously until a frost forms. Half fill a chilled tumbler with cracked ice cubes and strain the cocktail over them.
Piñata: put 4–6 cracked ice cubes into a cocktail shaker. Pour 2 measures golden tequila, 1 measure crème de banane and 1½ measures lime juice over the ice and shake vigorously until a frost forms. Strain the mixture into a chilled cocktail glass.

Crocodile

This is certainly a snappy cocktail with a bit of bite. However, it probably gets its name from its spectacular colour, created by the addition of Midori, a Japanese melon-flavoured liqueur, which is a startling shade of green.

serves 1

4–6 cracked ice cubes

2 measures vodka

1 measure triple sec

1 measure Midori

2 measures lemon juice

❶ Put the cracked ice cubes into a cocktail shaker. Pour the vodka, triple sec, Midori and lemon juice over the ice. Shake vigorously until a frost forms.

❷ Strain into a chilled cocktail glass.

Variations

Alligator: put 4–6 cracked ice cubes into a cocktail shaker. Pour 2 measures vodka, 1 measure Midori, ½ measure dry vermouth and ¼ teaspoon lemon juice over the ice. Shake vigorously until a frost forms. Strain into a chilled cocktail glass.

Melon Ball: put 4–6 cracked ice cubes into a mixing glass. Pour 2 measures vodka, 2 measures Midori and 4 measures pineapple juice over the ice and stir well to mix. Half fill a chilled tumbler with cracked ice cubes and strain the cocktail over them. Decorate with a melon wedge.

Melon Balls: put 4–6 cracked ice cubes into a cocktail shaker. Pour 1 measure vodka, 1 measure Midori and 1 measure pineapple juice over the ice. Shake vigorously until a frost forms, then strain into a chilled cocktail glass.

Melon State Balls: put 4–6 cracked ice cubes into a cocktail shaker. Pour 2 measures vodka, 1 measure Midori and 2 measures orange juice over the ice cubes. Shake vigorously until a frost forms, then strain the mixture into a chilled cocktail glass.

Vodga

As a rule, classic cocktails based on vodka were intended to provide the kick of an alcoholic drink with no tell-tale signs on the breath, and they were usually fairly simple mixes of fruit juice, sodas and other non-alcoholic flavourings. By contrast, contemporary cocktails based on vodka often include other aromatic and flavoursome spirits and liqueurs, with vodka adding extra strength.

serves 1

4–6 cracked ice cubes

2 measures vodka

1 measure Strega

½ measure orange juice

❶ Put the cracked ice cubes into a cocktail shaker. Pour the vodka, Strega and orange juice over the ice. Shake vigorously until a frost forms.

❷ Strain into a chilled cocktail glass.

Variations

Golden Frog: put 4–6 crushed ice cubes into a blender or food processor and add 1 measure vodka, 1 measure Strega, 1 measure Galliano and 1 measure lemon juice. Blend until slushy. Pour into a chilled cocktail glass.

Genoese: put 4–6 cracked ice cubes into a cocktail shaker. Pour 1 measure vodka, 1 measure grappa, ½ measure Sambuca and ½ measure dry vermouth over the ice. Shake vigorously until a frost forms, then strain into a chilled cocktail glass.

White Spider: put 4–6 cracked ice cubes into a mixing glass. Pour 1 measure vodka and 1 measure white crème de menthe over the ice. Stir well to mix, then strain into a chilled cocktail glass.

Tailgate: put 4–6 cracked ice cubes into a mixing glass. Dash orange bitters over the ice and pour in 2 measures vodka, 1 measure green Chartreuse and 1 measure sweet vermouth. Stir well to mix, then strain into a chilled cocktail glass.

Full Monty

The expression 'full monty', meaning not holding anything back, has been around for a long time, but was given a new lease of life by the highly successful British film of the same title. However, you can keep your clothes on when mixing and drinking this cocktail.

serves 1

4–6 cracked ice cubes
1 measure vodka
1 measure Galliano
grated ginseng root, to decorate

❶ Put the cracked ice cubes into a cocktail shaker. Pour the vodka and Galliano over the ice. Shake vigorously until a frost forms.

❷ Strain into a chilled cocktail glass and sprinkle with grated ginseng root.

Cinematic cocktails

Back to the Future: put 4–6 cracked ice cubes into a cocktail shaker. Pour 2 measures gin, 1 measure slivovitz and 1 measure lemon juice over the ice. Shake vigorously until a frost forms. Strain into a chilled cocktail glass.

Star Wars: put 4–6 cracked ice cubes into a cocktail shaker. Pour 2 measures gin, 2 measures lemon juice, 1 measure Galliano and 1 measure crème de noyaux over the ice. Shake vigorously until a frost forms. Strain into a chilled cocktail glass.

Titanic: put 4–6 cracked ice cubes into a cocktail shaker. Pour 3 measures Mandarine Napoléon and 2 measures vodka over the ice. Shake vigorously until a frost forms. Half fill a chilled tumbler with cracked ice cubes and strain the cocktail over them. Top up with sparkling mineral water.

Last Mango in Paris: put 4–6 cracked ice cubes into a blender or food processor and add 2 measures vodka, 1 measure crème de framboise, 1 measure lime juice, ½ peeled and chopped mango and 2 halved fresh strawberries. Blend until slushy. Pour into a chilled goblet. Decorate with a lime slice and a strawberry.

What the Hell

Cheer yourself up when you are at a loose end, or when everything seems to have gone wrong, with this simple but delicious concoction.

serves 1

4–6 cracked ice cubes
dash of lime juice
1 measure gin
1 measure apricot brandy
1 measure dry vermouth
lemon peel twist, to decorate

❶ Put the cracked ice cubes into a mixing glass. Dash the lime juice over the ice and pour in the gin, apricot brandy and vermouth. Stir well to mix.

❷ Strain into a chilled cocktail glass and decorate with a lemon peel twist.

Silly questions and answers

Why Not: put 4–6 cracked ice cubes into a mixing glass. Dash lemon juice over the ice. Pour in 2 measures gin, 1 measure peach brandy and 1 measure Noilly Prat. Stir to mix. Strain into a chilled cocktail glass.

Is This All: put 4–6 cracked ice cubes into a cocktail shaker. Pour 2 measures lemon vodka, 1 measure triple sec and 1 measure lemon juice over the ice and add 1 egg white. Shake until a frost forms. Strain into a chilled cocktail glass.

What the Dickens: pour 2 measures .gin into a heatproof tumbler and stir in 1½ teaspoons icing sugar. Top up with hot water.

This Is It: put 4–6 cracked ice cubes into a cocktail shaker. Pour 2 measures gin, 1 measure triple sec and 1 measure lemon juice over the ice and add 1 egg white. Shake vigorously until a frost forms. Strain the mixture into a chilled cocktail glass.

Did you know?

French vermouth, of which Noilly Prat is the leading brand, is almost always dry, whereas sweet red vermouth is still the most popular type in Italy, although all the well-known brands – Martini, Cinzano and Gancia – also include a dry version. Each firm keeps its own formula secret.

Non-alcoholic Cocktails

Lip Smacker

So many delicious ingredients are available today that non-alcoholic cocktails really have come into their own. This one has all the kick of an alcoholic cocktail.

serves 1

4–6 crushed ice cubes
1 small tomato, peeled, deseeded
and chopped
1 measure orange juice
2 tsp lime juice
1 spring onion, chopped
1 small fresh red chilli, deseeded
and chopped
pinch of caster sugar
pinch of salt
dash of Tabasco sauce

To decorate

lime slice
fresh chilli rosette (see below)

❶ Put the crushed ice, tomato, orange juice, lime juice, spring onion and chilli into a blender or food processor and process until smooth.
❷ Pour into a chilled glass and stir in the sugar, salt and Tabasco sauce. Decorate with a lime slice and a chilli rosette. To make a rosette, use a sharp knife to make 5 or 6 cuts 1 cm/½ inch from the stalk end to the tip of a long, thin chilli. Place in iced water for 30 minutes, until fanned out.

Variations

Hot Lips: substitute the flesh of ¼ small avocado for the tomato and a deseeded and chopped green chilli for the red chilli.
Open Prairie Oyster: dash Tabasco sauce and white wine vinegar into a wine glass and pour in 1 teaspoon Worcestershire sauce and 1 measure tomato juice. Stir gently and add 1 egg yolk. Drink down in one, without breaking the egg yolk.

Did you know?

Sun-ripened tomatoes have a much sweeter and more concentrated flavour than those grown under glass or in polytunnels. Home-grown varieties are best, but those sold on the vine are a good buy.

Little Prince

Sparkling apple juice is a particularly useful ingredient in non-alcoholic cocktails because it adds flavour and colour, as well as fizz. Try using it as a substitute for champagne in non-alcoholic versions of such cocktails as Buck's Fizz (see page 66).

serves 1

4–6 cracked ice cubes

1 measure apricot juice

1 measure lemon juice

2 measures sparkling apple juice

lemon peel twist, to decorate

❶ Put the cracked ice cubes into a mixing glass. Pour the apricot juice, lemon juice and apple juice over the ice and stir well.

❷ Strain into a chilled highball glass and decorate with the lemon peel twist.

An apple a day

Apple Frazzle: put 4–6 cracked ice cubes into a cocktail shaker. Pour 4 measures apple juice, 1 teaspoon sugar syrup (see page 11) and ½ teaspoon lemon juice over the ice. Shake vigorously until a frost forms. Strain into a chilled tumbler and top up with sparkling mineral water.

Bite of the Apple: put 4–6 crushed ice cubes into a blender or food processor and add 5 measures apple juice, 1 measure lime juice, ½ teaspoon orgeat and 1 tablespoon apple sauce or purée. Blend until smooth. Pour into a chilled tumbler. Sprinkle with ground cinnamon.

Prohibition Punch (to serve 25): pour 850 ml/1½ pints apple juice, 350 ml/ 12 fl oz lemon juice and 125 ml/4 fl oz sugar syrup (see page 11) into a large jug. Add cracked ice cubes and 2.5 litres/ 4½ pints ginger ale. Stir gently to mix. Serve in chilled tumblers, decorated with orange slices and with straws.

Red Apple Sunset: put 4–6 cracked ice cubes into a cocktail shaker. Dash grenadine over the ice and pour in 2 measures apple juice and 2 measures grapefruit juice. Shake until a frost forms. Strain into a chilled cocktail glass.

Grapefruit Cooler

This is a wonderfully refreshing drink that is ideal for serving at a family barbecue. Start making this at least two hours before you want to serve it to allow plenty of time for the mint to infuse in the syrup.

serves 6

55 g/2 oz fresh mint

2 measures sugar syrup (see page 11)

475 ml/17 fl oz grapefruit juice

4 measures lemon juice

about 30 cracked ice cubes

sparkling mineral water, to top up

fresh mint sprigs, to decorate

❶ Crush the fresh mint leaves and place in a small bowl. Add the sugar syrup and stir well. Leave to stand for at least 2 hours to macerate, mashing the mint with a spoon from time to time.

❷ Strain the syrup into a jug and add the grapefruit juice and lemon juice. Cover with clingfilm and chill in the refrigerator for at least 2 hours, until required.

❸ To serve, fill 6 chilled Collins glasses with cracked ice cubes. Divide the cocktail between the glasses and top up with sparkling mineral water. Decorate with fresh mint sprigs.

Cool it

Bright Green Cooler (to serve 1): put 4–6 cracked ice cubes into a cocktail shaker. Pour 3 measures pineapple juice, 2 measures lime juice and 1 measure green peppermint syrup over the ice. Shake the mixture vigorously until a frost forms. Half fill a tall, chilled tumbler with cracked ice cubes and strain the cocktail over them. Top up with ginger ale and then decorate with a cucumber slice and a lime slice.

Did you know?

There is a green-skinned grapefruit variety called 'Sweetie' that is less sharp than the yellow-skinned fruits. Pink grapefruit is also slightly milder in flavour.

Shirley Temple

This is one of the most famous of classic non-alcoholic cocktails. Shirley Temple
Black became a respected diplomat, but this cocktail dates from the days when
she was an immensely popular child film star in the 1930s.

serves 1

8–10 cracked ice cubes

2 measures lemon juice

½ measure grenadine

½ measure sugar syrup (see page 11)

ginger ale, to top up

To decorate

orange slice

maraschino cherry

❶ Put 4–6 cracked ice cubes into a
cocktail shaker. Pour the lemon juice,
grenadine and sugar syrup over the ice
and shake vigorously.

❷ Half fill a small, chilled glass with
cracked ice cubes and strain the
cocktail over them. Top up with ginger
ale. Decorate with an orange slice,
and a maraschino cherry speared on a
cocktail stick.

Other classics

St Clements: put 6–8 cracked ice cubes
into a chilled tumbler. Pour 2 measures
orange juice and 2 measures bitter lemon
over the ice. Stir gently and decorate with
orange and lemon slices.

Black and Tan: pour 150 ml/5 fl oz
chilled ginger ale into a chilled tumbler.
Add 150 ml/5 fl oz chilled ginger beer. Do
not stir. Decorate with a lime wedge.

Tea Punch: put 4–6 cracked ice cubes
into a mixing glass. Pour 3 measures cold
black tea, 3 measures orange juice,
3 measures sparkling apple juice and
1½ measures lemon juice over the ice. Stir
well to mix, then pour into a tall, chilled
tumbler. Decorate with a lemon slice.

Beachcomber: put 4–6 cracked ice cubes
into a cocktail shaker. Pour 150 ml/5 fl oz
guava juice, 2 measures lime juice and
1 measure raspberry syrup over the ice.
Shake vigorously until a frost forms. Pour
into a chilled tumbler.

Melon Medley

Choose a very ripe, sweet-fleshed melon, such as a cantaloupe, for this lovely, fresh-tasting cocktail. This drink is perfect for sipping on a hot evening.

serves 1

4–6 crushed ice cubes
55 g/2 oz diced melon flesh
4 measures orange juice
½ measure lemon juice

❶ Put the crushed ice into a blender or food processor and add the diced melon. Pour in the orange juice and lemon juice. Blend until slushy.
❷ Pour into a chilled Collins glass.

Sweet and juicy

River Cruise (to serve 6): put 450 g/1 lb diced cantaloupe melon flesh into a blender or food processor and process to a smooth purée. Scrape into a jug. Put the grated rind and juice of 2 lemons and 2 tablespoons sugar into a small saucepan. Heat gently, stirring until the sugar has dissolved. Pour the lemon syrup over the melon purée and leave to cool, then cover with clingfilm and chill in the refrigerator for at least 2 hours. To serve, half fill 6 chilled tumblers with cracked ice.

Stir the melon mixture and divide it between the glasses. Top up with sparkling mineral water and decorate with melon wedges and maraschino cherries.

Kool Kevin: put 4–6 crushed ice cubes into a blender or food processor and add 55 g/2 oz diced cantaloupe melon flesh, 1 measure grenadine and 1 measure double cream. Blend until smooth. Pour into a chilled glass. Add 1 measure ginger ale and stir gently. Sprinkle with ground ginger and decorate with a melon wedge.

Smoothies

& Juices

It is no surprise that smoothies and mixed juices have become so fashionable in these health-conscious days. Commercial soft drinks and even some fruit juices often contain ingredients that many of us would rather avoid – artificial colourings and flavourings, high levels of sugar or chemical sweeteners and preservatives. In addition, many of them are so sickly, bland

or unexciting that they simply do not appeal to the adult palate. Making fruit and vegetable drinks at home ensures that we know precisely what they contain. It also means that we can mix them to taste truly delicious. What is more, we can guarantee that the raw ingredients are organic, if that's what we want.

Nutritionists recommend that we should eat at least five portions of fruit and vegetables a day. Modern life is so busy, however, that few of us have the time or inclination to plan, shop, prepare and cook balanced meals every day of the week. The good news is that in the few minutes it takes to juice a handful of carrots and tomatoes, or to whizz some berries and yogurt in the food

processor, we can produce the equivalent of one of those portions. Better still, the ingredients are usually raw and the juice or smoothie will be consumed immediately. So there is less possibility of nutrients leaching out during cooking or being destroyed through excessive exposure to air. This makes the drink even healthier.

You can make smoothies and juices from most fruit and vegetables. The golden rule is never to combine the two, with the exceptions of apples and carrots, which go with just about everything, and tomatoes, a fruit that most treat as a vegetable. The following recipes will give you an excellent starting point, and should provide you with lots of ideas for inventing your own drinks. Generally, once people have begun the habit of making their own fruit and vegetable drinks, they become great enthusiasts and never feel the need to return to commercial brands.

Of course, smoothies and juices are very enjoyable thirst-quenchers, but there is much more to them than this. Many provide a powerful boost that can kick-start the day at breakfast time or revive flagging energy in the afternoon, with a healthy nutritional balance that you won't find in a packet of biscuits or a chocolate bar. Bananas, for example, are full of natural sugar, which provides a source of rapidly released energy. Citrus fruits, berries and, above all, kiwi fruit are packed with vitamin C; strawberries and

raspberries contain iron; and carrots are a valuable source of betacarotene. In addition, with a juicer (see page 102), fibre is incorporated in the drink and not discarded.

The following recipes are divided into three sections – Fruits, Vegetables, Herbs & Spices and Sweets & Coffees. The selection of delicious drinks does not only include smoothies and mixed juices, but also coolers and other long drinks; pick-me-ups; tea- and coffee-based mixes; and some lovely milkshakes for a special treat. You will also find some useful information about equipment and ways of preparing ingredients to set you on the right path to complete success in making your own healthy and tasty fruit and vegetable concoctions.

Equipment

Making smoothies and juices is great fun, as well as being very healthy. All you need is the right equipment and ingredients, some recipes and your imagination. You don't have to spend a lot of money on equipment, but for the best and freshest results, you will need a food processor and a juicer.

A basic kitchen food processor with a standard metal blade mixes smoothies to perfection in a few moments, and the following recipes assume that one will be used. You might also be able to use a blender, depending on how robust the model is. However, unless your food processor has a juicer attachment, you cannot use it for making juice, because it will just turn the ingredients into a purée. A juicer, on the other hand, separates the pulp from the juice. There are three types of juicer, and these vary considerably in price. Centrifugal juicers are at the lower end of the price range. Coarsely chopped ingredients are fed into this type of machine, which grates them into tiny pieces and spins them at high speed. The liquid is extracted by centrifugal force, leaving the fruit or vegetable pulp behind. As the fruit and vegetables are exposed to the air throughout the process, juices made by this method are thought to have the lowest nutritional content.

Hydraulic juicers are at the top end of the price range. Extreme pressure forces the juice out of the ingredients, through a strainer and into a jug, leaving the pulp behind. Juices pressed by this method are very high in nutrients.

The third type, triturating juicers, are in the middle of the price range and the juice they produce is in the middle of the nutritional range. A rotating cutter tears up the ingredients and simultaneously presses them against a strainer.

Besides cost, other aspects to consider before buying a juicer are size – triturating juicers tend to be larger than the others – the speed at which they work and how easy they are to clean. But whichever type of juicer you choose, you can still be sure that the drink you are creating will be full of nutrients as well as flavour.

Any other equipment you are likely need, from a chopping board to an ice-cube tray, you will almost certainly already have in your kitchen cupboards. You should never use a chopping board used for meat for preparing fruit and vegetables.

Techniques

When you use a food processor, everything that goes into the bowl will be incorporated into the final drink. Consequently, fruit and vegetables must be washed, peeled and prepared in just the same way as for any other type of recipe. Stones, pips and seeds must all be removed. Large, firm fruit and vegetables, such as apples and carrots, should be roughly chopped before being placed in the processor.

If you are going to add ice cubes to the food processor, they need to be crushed before they are added. See page 11 for instructions on how to crush ice.

The technique with juicers, whatever type you are using, is different because the juice and solid residue are kept separate. Most vegetables and fruits, with the obvious exceptions of bananas, kiwi fruit and citrus fruits, do not need to be peeled. However, it is still important that they are thoroughly washed.

Some juicers can cope with quite tough skins, even including the skins of melons. Many of the nutrients in fruits lie just below the surface of the skin, so this is a particularly valuable asset, but it does mean that you must be sure to use specimens with undamaged skin.

As a rough guide to making your own fresh juices, 500 g/1 lb 2 oz of raw carrots or apples yields 225 ml/8 fl oz of juice, while 500 g/ 1 lb 2 oz of tomatoes or blackberries will produce 325 ml/11 fl oz of fresh juice.

You can leave vegetable tops, such as beetroot leaves, attached, but do trim off the roots. Coarse outer leaves that would be removed for other culinary purposes don't need trimming. Stones, such as those in cherries, peaches and mangoes, should be removed, but you can leave smaller seeds and pips in grapes, apples and pears. Then the process of actually making the juice is very simple.

Fruits

Melon Smoothie

This summer smoothie, with three different kinds of melon, is deliciously refreshing on a hot day.

serves 2

250 ml/9 fl oz natural yogurt

100 g/3½ oz galia melon, peeled, deseeded and cut into chunks

100 g/3½ oz cantaloupe melon, peeled, deseeded and cut into chunks

100 g/3½ oz watermelon, peeled, deseeded and cut into chunks

6 ice cubes

melon wedges, to decorate

Method

❶ Pour the yogurt into a food processor. Add the galia melon chunks and process until smooth.

❷ Add the cantaloupe and watermelon chunks along with the ice cubes and process until smooth. Pour the mixture into 2 glasses and decorate with melon wedges. Serve immediately.

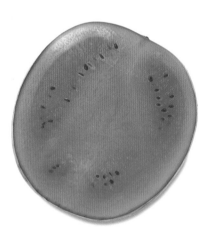

Nectarine Melt

Mango and nectarine is an inspired combination, made all the more special with the clever addition of lemon sorbet.

serves 2

250 ml/9 fl oz milk

350 g/12 oz lemon sorbet

1 ripe mango, peeled, stoned and diced

2 ripe nectarines, peeled, stoned and diced

Method

❶ Pour the milk into a food processor, add half the lemon sorbet and process gently until combined. Add the remaining sorbet and process until smooth.

❷ When the mixture is thoroughly blended, gradually add the mango and nectarines and process until smooth. Pour the mixture into 2 glasses and add straws, then serve.

Orange & Lime Iced Tea

Sweet and sharp citrus flavours turn a very simple drink into a subtle and sophisticated thirst-quencher.

serves 2

300 ml/10 fl oz water

2 tea bags

100 ml/3½ fl oz orange juice

4 tbsp lime juice

1–2 tbsp brown sugar

8 ice cubes

To decorate

lime wedge

granulated sugar

orange, lemon or lime slices

Method

❶ Pour the water into a saucepan and bring to the boil. Remove the saucepan from the heat, then add the tea bags and leave to infuse for 5 minutes. Remove the tea bags and leave the tea to cool for 30 minutes, or until room temperature. Transfer to a jug, then cover with clingfilm and chill in the refrigerator for at least 45 minutes.

❷ When the tea has chilled, pour in the orange juice and lime juice. Add brown sugar to taste.

❸ Take 2 glasses and rub the rims with a lime wedge, then dip them in granulated sugar to frost. Put the ice cubes into the glasses and pour over the tea. Decorate the rims with orange, lemon or lime slices and serve.

Fruit Cooler

Power up with breakfast in a glass, packed with protein and vitamins – and a sensational flavour, too.

serves 2

250 ml/9 fl oz orange juice

125 ml/4 fl oz natural yogurt

2 eggs

2 bananas, peeled, sliced and frozen

fresh banana slices, to decorate

Method

❶ Pour the orange juice and yogurt into a food processor and process gently until combined.

❷ Add the eggs and frozen banana slices and process until smooth. Pour the mixture into 2 glasses and decorate the rims with banana slices. Add straws and serve.

Spicy Banana Chill

A Caribbean combo to tantalize the taste buds with just a hint of heat in every mouthful of icy sweetness.

serves 2

300 ml/10 fl oz milk

½ tsp mixed spice

150 g/5½ oz banana ice cream

2 bananas, peeled, sliced and frozen

Method

❶ Pour the milk into a food processor and add the mixed spice. Add half the banana ice cream and process gently until combined, then add the remaining ice cream and process until well blended.

❷ When the mixture is well combined, add the frozen banana slices and process until smooth. Pour the mixture into 2 tall glasses and add straws, then serve immediately.

Cranberry Energizer

Top up your vitamin C levels – this is the perfect pick-me-up for getting going and waking up a sluggish system.

serves 2

300 ml/10 fl oz cranberry juice

100 ml/3½ fl oz orange juice

150 g/5½ oz fresh raspberries

1 tbsp lemon juice

lemon or orange slices and spirals, to decorate

Method

❶ Pour the cranberry juice and orange juice into a food processor and process gently until combined. Add the raspberries and lemon juice and process until smooth.

❷ Pour the mixture into 2 glasses and decorate with lemon or orange slices and spirals speared on a cocktail stick. Serve immediately.

Caribbean Cocktail

Chill out with a tropical treat. If you close your eyes, you can almost hear the waves lapping on the beach.

serves 2

100 ml/3½ fl oz coconut milk

200 ml/7 fl oz soya milk

100 ml/3½ fl oz pineapple juice

1 tbsp brown sugar

1 ripe mango, peeled, stoned and diced

2 tbsp grated fresh coconut

140 g/5 oz frozen pineapple chunks

1 banana, peeled, sliced and frozen

To decorate

grated fresh coconut

fresh pineapple wedges

Method

❶ Put the coconut milk, soya milk, pineapple juice and sugar into a food processor and process gently until combined. Add the diced mango to the food processor along with the grated coconut and process well.

❷ Add the frozen pineapple chunks and banana slices and process until smooth. Pour the mixture into 2 glasses, then sprinkle over some grated coconut and decorate the rims with fresh pineapple wedges. Serve immediately.

Pineapple Soda

Ice cream soda for grown-ups, this luscious mix of pineapple, coconut milk and
vanilla ice cream is irresistible.

serves 2

175 ml/6 fl oz pineapple juice

100 ml/3½ fl oz coconut milk

200 g/7 oz vanilla ice cream

140 g/5 oz frozen pineapple chunks

175 ml/6 fl oz sparkling mineral water

2 scooped-out pineapple shells

(optional)

Method

❶ Pour the pineapple juice and coconut milk into a food processor. Add the ice cream and process until smooth.

❷ Add the frozen pineapple chunks and process well. Pour the mixture into 2 scooped-out pineapple shells or tall glasses until two-thirds full. Top up with sparkling mineral water, then add straws and serve.

Pineapple & Coconut Shake

The perfect partnership – and a lovely way to wind down at the end of a busy day
with your own perfect partner.

serves 2

350 ml/12 fl oz pineapple juice

100 ml/3½ fl oz coconut milk

150 g/5½ oz vanilla ice cream

140 g/5 oz frozen pineapple chunks

2 scooped-out coconut shells
(optional)

2 tbsp grated fresh coconut, to decorate

Method

❶ Pour the pineapple juice and coconut milk into a food processor. Add the ice cream and process until smooth.

❷ Add the frozen pineapple chunks and process until smooth. Pour the mixture into 2 scooped-out coconut shells or tall glasses and decorate with grated coconut. Add straws and serve.

Peach & Pineapple Smoothie

Sweet and creamy with a hint of sharpness, this elegant smoothie will appeal to sophisticated palates.

serves 2

125 ml/4 fl oz pineapple juice

juice of 1 lemon

100 ml/3½ fl oz water

3 tbsp brown sugar

175 ml/6 fl oz natural yogurt

1 ripe peach, peeled, stoned, cut into chunks and frozen

100 g/3½ oz frozen pineapple chunks

fresh pineapple wedges, to decorate

Method

❶ Pour the pineapple juice, lemon juice and water into a food processor. Add the sugar and yogurt and process until blended.

❷ Add the frozen peach and pineapple chunks and process until smooth. Pour the mixture into 2 glasses and decorate the rims with pineapple wedges. Serve immediately.

Pineapple Crush

A long, cool thirst-quencher, this will boost your concentration and revitalize a tired or stressed mind.

serves 2

100 ml/3½ fl oz pineapple juice

4 tbsp orange juice

115 g/4 oz galia melon, peeled, deseeded
and cut into chunks

140 g/5 oz frozen pineapple chunks

4 ice cubes

To decorate

galia melon slices

orange slices

Method

❶ Pour the pineapple juice and orange juice into a food processor and process gently until combined.

❷ Add the melon, frozen pineapple chunks and ice cubes and process until a slushy consistency has been reached.

❸ Pour the mixture into 2 glasses and decorate with melon and orange slices. Serve immediately.

Hawaiian Shake

When your energy levels are flagging, give yourself a treat with this invigorating
and exuberant shake.

serves 2

250 ml/9 fl oz milk

50 ml/2 fl oz coconut milk

150 g/5½ oz vanilla ice cream

2 bananas, peeled, sliced and frozen

200 g/7 oz canned pineapple chunks,
drained

1 ripe pawpaw, peeled, deseeded and diced

To decorate

grated fresh coconut

fresh pineapple wedges

Method

❶ Pour the milk and coconut milk into a food processor and process gently until combined. Add half the ice cream and process gently, then add the remaining ice cream and process until smooth.

❷ Add the frozen banana slices and process well, then add the pineapple chunks and pawpaw and process until smooth. Pour the mixture into 2 tall glasses, then sprinkle over the grated fresh coconut and decorate the rims with pineapple wedges. Serve immediately.

Pacific Smoothie

Luscious figs combine superbly with the nuts, orange juice and maple syrup in this unusual and delicate drink.

serves 2

350 ml/12 fl oz hazelnut yogurt

2 tbsp freshly squeezed orange juice

4 tbsp maple syrup

8 large fresh figs, peeled and chopped

6 ice cubes

toasted chopped hazelnuts, to decorate

Method

❶ Pour the yogurt, orange juice and maple syrup into a food processor and process gently until combined.

❷ Add the figs and ice cubes and process until smooth. Pour the mixture into 2 glasses and sprinkle over some toasted chopped hazelnuts. Serve immediately.

Rose Sunset

This beautifully fragrant drink, with its romantic name, has an equally delectable and illusive flavour.

serves 2

100 ml/3½ fl oz natural yogurt

500 ml/18 fl oz milk

1 tbsp rosewater

3 tbsp honey

1 ripe mango, peeled, stoned and diced

6 ice cubes

edible rose petals, to decorate (optional)

Method

❶ Pour the yogurt and milk into a food processor and process gently until combined.

❷ Add the rosewater and honey and process until thoroughly blended, then add the mango along with the ice cubes and process until smooth. Pour the mixture into 2 glasses, then decorate with edible rose petals, if desired, and serve.

Fruit Rapture

Simple, but splendid, this restorative smoothie will get you back on track at any time of day.

serves 2

100 ml/3½ fl oz milk

125 ml/4 fl oz peach yogurt

100 ml/3½ fl oz orange juice

225 g/8 oz canned peach slices, drained

6 ice cubes

orange peel strips, to decorate

Method

❶ Pour the milk, yogurt and orange juice into a food processor and process gently until combined.

❷ Add the peach slices and ice cubes and process until smooth. Pour the mixture into 2 glasses and decorate with orange peel strips. Add straws and serve.

Traditional Lemonade

A classic cooler that is redolent of a more leisured and peaceful era, this is a well-loved favourite.

serves 2

150 ml/5 fl oz water

6 tbsp sugar

1 tsp grated lemon rind

125 ml/4 fl oz lemon juice

6 ice cubes

sparkling mineral water

To decorate

lemon wedge

granulated sugar

lemon slices

Method

❶ Put the water, sugar and grated lemon rind into a small saucepan and bring to the boil, stirring constantly. Continue to boil, stirring, for 5 minutes.

❷ Remove the saucepan from the heat and leave to cool for 30 minutes, or until room temperature. Stir in the lemon juice, then transfer to a jug and cover with clingfilm. Chill in the refrigerator for at least 2 hours.

❸ When the lemon mixture has almost finished chilling, take 2 glasses and rub the rims with a lemon wedge, then dip them in granulated sugar to frost. Put the ice cubes into the glasses.

❹ Remove the mixture from the refrigerator, then pour it over the ice and top up with sparkling mineral water. The ratio should be 1 part lemon mixture to 3 parts sparkling mineral water. Stir well to mix. Decorate with lemon slices and serve.

Kiwi Dream

More than a whole day's dose of vitamin C in a glass, as well as a wonderfully refreshing sweet and sharp flavour.

serves 2

150 ml/5 fl oz milk

juice of 2 limes

2 kiwi fruit, peeled and chopped

1 tbsp sugar

400 g/14 oz vanilla ice cream

To decorate

kiwi fruit slices

lime peel strips

Method

❶ Pour the milk and lime juice into a food processor and process gently until combined.

❷ Add the kiwi fruit and sugar and process gently, then add the ice cream and process until smooth. Pour the mixture into 2 glasses and decorate with kiwi fruit slices and lime peel strips. Serve immediately.

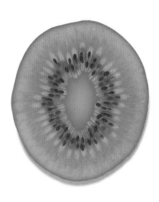

Banana & Apple Booster

Kick-start your day and wake up your taste buds with this zingy vitamin- and mineral-packed energizer.

serves 2

250 ml/9 fl oz apple juice

½ tsp ground cinnamon

2 tsp grated fresh root ginger

2 bananas, peeled, sliced and frozen

fresh banana slices,

to decorate

Method

❶ Pour the apple juice into a food processor. Add the cinnamon and ginger and process gently until combined.

❷ Add the frozen banana slices and process until smooth. Pour the mixture into 2 tall glasses and decorate with banana slices speared on cocktail sticks. Serve immediately.

Banana & Blueberry Smoothie

Sweet, sharp, fragrant, rich and creamy, this is pure magic-in-a-glass that will lift your spirits.

serves 2

175 ml/6 fl oz apple juice

125 ml/4 fl oz natural yogurt

1 banana, peeled, sliced and frozen

175 g/6 oz frozen blueberries

whole fresh blueberries, to decorate

Method

❶ Pour the apple juice into a food processor. Add the yogurt and process until smooth.

❷ Add the frozen banana slices and half the frozen blueberries and process well, then add the remaining blueberries and process until smooth. Pour the mixture into 2 tall glasses and decorate with whole blueberries. Add straws and serve.

Raspberry Cooler

Liquid sunshine – not only is this superbly refreshing, but it also tones the whole system.

serves 2

8 crushed ice cubes

2 tbsp raspberry syrup

500 ml/18 fl oz chilled apple juice

To decorate

whole fresh raspberries

apple pieces

Method

❶ Divide the crushed ice between 2 glasses. Pour the raspberry syrup over the ice.

❷ Top up each glass with chilled apple juice and stir well. Decorate with the whole raspberries and apple pieces speared on cocktail sticks and serve.

Berry Cream

The inspired combination of sweet banana and tart summer berries could almost be described as intoxicating.

serves 2

350 ml/12 fl oz orange juice

450 g/1 lb frozen forest fruits (such as blueberries, raspberries and blackberries)

1 banana, peeled, sliced and frozen

fresh strawberry slices, to decorate

Method

❶ Pour the orange juice into a food processor. Add half the frozen forest fruits and the banana slices and process until smooth.

❷ Add the remaining forest fruits and process until smooth. Pour the mixture into 2 tall glasses and decorate the rims with strawberry slices. Add straws and serve.

Strawberry & Orange Smoothie

Probably one of the first smoothies ever invented, this impeccable combination remains a firm favourite.

serves 2

125 ml/4 fl oz natural yogurt

175 ml/6 fl oz strawberry yogurt

175 ml/6 fl oz orange juice

175 g/6 oz frozen strawberries

1 banana, peeled, sliced and frozen

To decorate

orange slices

whole fresh strawberries

Method

❶ Pour the natural and strawberry yogurts into a food processor and process gently. Add the orange juice and process until the mixture is combined.

❷ Add the frozen strawberries and banana slices and process until smooth. Pour the mixture into 2 tall glasses and decorate with orange slices and whole strawberries. Add straws and serve.

Strawberry & Peach Smoothie

One luscious glassful of this wonderfully fruity mix and you will feel restored, revived and refreshed.

serves 2

175 ml/6 fl oz milk

225 g/8 oz canned peach slices, drained

2 ripe apricots, peeled, stoned and chopped

400 g/14 oz fresh strawberries, hulled and sliced

2 bananas, peeled, sliced and frozen

fresh strawberry slices, to decorate

Method

❶ Pour the milk into a food processor. Add the peach slices and process gently until combined. Add the apricots and process gently until combined.

❷ Add the strawberries and frozen banana slices and process until smooth. Pour the mixture into 2 glasses and decorate the rims with strawberry slices. Add straws and serve immediately.

Summer & Citrus Fruit Punch

Serve this vibrant punch whenever you have something to celebrate, or just to make yourself feel good.

serves 2

4 tbsp orange juice

1 tbsp lime juice

100 ml/3½ fl oz sparkling mineral water

350 g/12 oz frozen summer fruits
(such as blueberries, raspberries,
blackberries and strawberries)

4 ice cubes

whole fresh raspberries, blackcurrants and
blackberries, to decorate

Method

❶ Pour the orange juice, lime juice and sparkling mineral water into a food processor. Process gently until combined.

❷ Add the frozen summer fruits and ice cubes and process until a slushy consistency has been reached. Pour the mixture into 2 glasses, decorate with raspberries, blackcurrants and blackberries speared on cocktail sticks and serve.

Cherry Kiss

This long and lively cooler is a welcome way to turn off the heat in the middle of summer.

serves 2

8 ice cubes, crushed

2 tbsp cherry syrup

500 ml/18 fl oz sparkling mineral water

maraschino cherries,
to decorate

Method

❶ Divide the crushed ice between 2 glasses. Pour the cherry syrup over the ice.

❷ Top up each glass with sparkling mineral water. Decorate with the maraschino cherries speared on cocktail sticks and serve.

Vegetables,
Herbs & Spices

Red Pepper Reactor

Boost your energy levels and fire up your system with this truly dynamic vegetable medley.

serves 2

250 ml/9 fl oz carrot juice

250 ml/9 fl oz tomato juice

2 large red peppers,
deseeded and roughly chopped

1 tbsp lemon juice

pepper, to serve

Method

❶ Pour the carrot juice and tomato juice into a food processor and process gently until combined.

❷ Add the red peppers and lemon juice. Season with plenty of pepper and process until smooth. Pour the mixture into 2 tall glasses, then add straws and serve immediately.

Ginger Crush

The sweet, mild flavours of carrot and tomato are literally gingered up
in this enlivening drink.

serves 2

250 ml/9 fl oz carrot juice

4 tomatoes, peeled, deseeded and
roughly chopped

1 tbsp lemon juice

25 g/1 oz fresh parsley

1 tbsp grated fresh root ginger

6 ice cubes

125 ml/4 fl oz water

chopped fresh parsley, to garnish

Method

❶ Put the carrot juice, tomatoes and
lemon juice into a food processor and
process gently until combined.

❷ Add the parsley to the food processor
along with the ginger and ice cubes.

Process until well combined, then pour
in the water and process until smooth.

❸ Pour the mixture into 2 tall glasses
and garnish with chopped parsley.
Serve immediately.

Peppermint Ice

Simultaneously hot and cold on the tongue, this classic combination still manages to surprise.

serves 2

150 ml/5 fl oz milk

2 tbsp peppermint syrup

400 g/14 oz peppermint ice cream

fresh mint sprigs, to decorate

Method

❶ Pour the milk and peppermint syrup into a food processor and process gently until combined.

❷ Add the peppermint ice cream and process until smooth. Pour the mixture into 2 tall glasses and decorate with mint. sprigs. Add straws and serve.

Cinnamon & Lemon Tea

Enjoy this aromatic winter warmer and, at the same time, keep the worst of the weather and colds at bay.

serves 2

400 ml/14 fl oz water

4 cloves

1 small cinnamon stick

2 tea bags

3–4 tbsp lemon juice

1–2 tbsp brown sugar

lemon slices, to decorate

Method

❶ Put the water, cloves and cinnamon into a saucepan and bring to the boil. Remove the saucepan from the heat and add the tea bags. Leave to infuse for 5 minutes, then remove the tea bags.

❷ Stir in lemon juice and sugar to taste. Return the saucepan to a low heat and warm through gently. Do not boil.

❸ Remove the saucepan from the heat and strain the tea into 2 heatproof glasses. Decorate with lemon slices and serve.

Celery Surprise

A savoury delight that not only acts as a tonic, but also cleanses and
refreshes the palate.

serves 2

125 ml/4 fl oz carrot juice

500 g/1 lb 2 oz tomatoes,
peeled, deseeded and roughly chopped

1 tbsp lemon juice

4 celery sticks, sliced

4 spring onions,
roughly chopped

25 g/1 oz fresh parsley

25 g/1 oz fresh mint

2 celery sticks, to garnish

Method

❶ Put the carrot juice, tomatoes and lemon juice into a food processor and process gently until combined.

❷ Add the sliced celery along with the spring onions, parsley and mint and process until smooth. Pour the mixture into 2 tall glasses and garnish with celery sticks. Serve immediately.

Curried Crush

Juice with attitude – this stimulating blend of flavours is guaranteed to add spice to your life.

serves 2

250 ml/9 fl oz carrot juice

4 tomatoes, peeled, deseeded and roughly chopped

1 tbsp lemon juice

2 celery sticks, sliced

1 cos lettuce

1 garlic clove, chopped

25 g/1 oz fresh parsley

1 tsp curry powder

6 ice cubes

125 ml/4 fl oz water

2 celery sticks, to garnish

Method

❶ Put the carrot juice, tomatoes, lemon juice and sliced celery into a food processor and process until combined.

❷ Separate the lettuce leaves, then wash them and add them to the food processor along with the garlic, parsley, curry powder and ice cubes. Process until well combined, then pour in the water and process until smooth.

❸ Pour the mixture into 2 tall glasses, garnish with celery sticks and serve.

Watercress Float

Peppery watercress perks up carrot juice and provides extra vitamins and minerals in this cleansing drink.

serves 2

500 ml/18 fl oz carrot juice

25 g/1 oz watercress

1 tbsp lemon juice

watercress sprigs, to garnish

Method

❶ Pour the carrot juice into a food processor. Add the watercress and lemon juice and process until smooth. Transfer to a jug, then cover with clingfilm and leave to chill in the refrigerator for at least 1 hour, or until required.

❷ When the mixture is thoroughly chilled, pour into 2 glasses and garnish with watercress sprigs. Serve immediately.

Orange & Carrot Smoothie

This doesn't just taste and look fabulous, but contains abundant, health-giving betacarotene and vitamin C.

serves 2

175 ml/6 fl oz carrot juice

175 ml/6 fl oz orange juice

150 g/5½ oz vanilla ice cream

6 ice cubes

To decorate

orange slices

orange peel strips

Method

❶ Pour the carrot juice and orange juice into a food processor and process gently until well combined. Add the ice cream and process until thoroughly blended.

❷ Add the ice cubes and process until smooth. Pour the mixture into 2 glasses, decorate with orange slices and orange peel strips and serve.

Red Storm

A sure-fire lip-smacker, this spicy little number is definitely not for the unwary or faint-hearted.

serves 2

500 ml/18 fl oz tomato juice

dash of Worcestershire sauce

1 small fresh red chilli,
deseeded and chopped

1 spring onion, chopped

6 ice cubes

2 long, thin fresh red chillies, cut into
flowers (see below), to garnish

Method

❶ To make the chilli flowers for the garnish, use a small sharp knife to make 6 cuts lengthways along each chilli. Place the tip of the knife about 1 cm/½ inch from the stalk end and cut towards the tip. Put the chillies into a bowl of iced water and leave them for 25–30 minutes, or until they have spread out into flower shapes.

❷ Put the tomato juice and Worcestershire sauce into a food processor and process gently until combined. Add the chopped chilli, spring onion and ice cubes and process until smooth.

❸ Pour the mixture into 2 glasses and garnish with the chilli flowers. Add straws and serve.

Sweets

& Coffees

Rich Chocolate Shake

The ultimate milkshake for children and chocoholics of all ages, this is
supremely satisfying.

serves 2

150 ml/5 fl oz milk

2 tbsp chocolate syrup

400 g/14 oz chocolate ice cream

grated chocolate, to decorate

Method

❶ Pour the milk and chocolate syrup into a food processor and process gently until combined.

❷ Add the chocolate ice cream and process until smooth. Pour the mixture into 2 tall glasses and sprinkle the grated chocolate over the top. Serve immediately.

Maple & Almond Milkshake

Go on. Why not indulge your sweet tooth with this rather grown-up, rich-tasting, novel milkshake?

serves 2

150 ml/5 fl oz milk

2 tbsp maple syrup

400 g/14 oz vanilla ice cream

1 tbsp almond essence

chopped almonds, to decorate

Method

1 Pour the milk and maple syrup into a food processor and process gently until combined.

2 Add the ice cream and almond essence and process until smooth. Pour the mixture into 2 tall glasses and decorate with chopped almonds. Add straws and serve.

Coffee Whip

The magical pairing of coffee and chocolate can be improved only by the addition of whipped cream.

serves 2

200 ml/7 fl oz milk

50 ml/2 fl oz single cream

1 tbsp brown sugar

2 tbsp cocoa powder

1 tbsp coffee syrup or

instant coffee powder

6 ice cubes

To decorate

whipped cream

grated chocolate

Method

❶ Put the milk, cream and sugar into a food processor and process gently until combined.

❷ Add the cocoa powder and coffee syrup or powder and process well, then add the ice cubes and process until smooth. Pour the mixture into 2 glasses. Top with whipped cream and sprinkle over the grated chocolate, then serve.

Banana & Coffee Milkshake

A powerhouse drink for those who lead life on the run, this unusual milkshake tastes great, too.

serves 2

300 ml/10 fl oz milk

4 tbsp instant coffee powder

150 g/5½ oz vanilla ice cream

2 bananas, peeled, sliced and frozen

Method

❶ Pour the milk into a food processor, then add the coffee powder and process gently until combined. Add half the vanilla ice cream and process gently, then add the remaining ice cream and process until well combined.

❷ When the mixture is thoroughly blended, add the frozen banana slices and process until smooth. Pour the mixture into 2 tall glasses and serve.

Smooth Iced Coffee

Nothing could be nicer after a long, lazy, alfresco lunch than this cool, elegant iced coffee.

serves 2

400 ml/14 fl oz water

2 tbsp instant coffee granules

2 tbsp brown sugar

6 ice cubes

To decorate

single cream

whole coffee beans

Method

❶ Use the water and coffee granules to brew some hot coffee, then leave to cool for 30 minutes, or until room temperature. Transfer to a jug, then cover with clingfilm and leave to chill in the refrigerator for at least 45 minutes.

❷ When the coffee has chilled, pour it into a food processor. Add the sugar and process until well combined. Add the ice cubes and process until smooth.

❸ Pour the mixture into 2 tall glasses. Float cream on the top and decorate with whole coffee beans, then serve.

Hazelnut & Coffee Sparkle

Try something a little different – you will be pleasantly surprised by how successful this mix is.

serves 2

250 ml/9 fl oz water

3 tbsp instant coffee granules

125 ml/4 fl oz sparkling mineral water

1 tbsp hazelnut syrup

2 tbsp brown sugar

6 ice cubes

To decorate

lime slices

lemon slices

Method

❶ Use the water and coffee granules to brew some hot coffee, then leave to cool for 30 minutes, or until room temperature. Transfer to a jug, then cover with clingfilm and leave to chill in the refrigerator for at least 45 minutes.

❷ When the coffee has chilled, pour it into a food processor. Add the sparkling mineral water, hazelnut syrup and sugar and process well. Add the ice cubes and process until smooth.

❸ Pour the mixture into 2 tall glasses and decorate the rims with lime and lemon slices, then serve.

Peppermint Mocha

This exhilarating fusion of flavours could certainly set tongues wagging – but only with sheer delight.

serves 2

400 ml/14 fl oz milk

200 ml/7 fl oz coffee syrup

100 ml/3½ fl oz peppermint syrup

1 tbsp chopped fresh mint leaves

4 ice cubes

To decorate

grated chocolate

fresh mint sprigs

Method

❶ Pour the milk, coffee syrup and peppermint syrup into a food processor and process gently until combined.

❷ Add the mint and ice cubes and process until a slushy consistency has been reached.

❸ Pour the mixture into 2 glasses. Sprinkle over the grated chocolate, and decorate with mint sprigs, then serve.

Drinks List

- Acapulco *44* • American Rose *20* • Banana & Apple Booster *140*
- Banana & Blueberry Smoothie *142* • Banana & Coffee Milkshake *184*
- Berry Cream *146* • Bloody Mary *58* • Buck's Fizz *66* • Caribbean Cocktail *118*
- Carolina *76* • Celery Surprise *166* • Cherry Kiss *154* • Cinnamon & Lemon Tea *164*
- Classic Cocktail *14* • Coffee Whip *182* • Cranberry Energizer *116* • Crocodile *78*
- Cuba Libre *48* • Curried Crush *168* • Daiquiri *46* • Frozen Daiquiri *70*
- Fruit Cooler *112* • Fruit Rapture *134* • Full Monty *82* • Ginger Crush *160*
- Grapefruit Cooler *92* • Hawaiian Shake *128* • Hazelnut & Coffee Sparkle *188*
- Kir *64* • Kiwi Dream *138* • Lip Smacker *88* • Little Prince *90*
- Long Island Iced Tea *40* • Mai Tai *52* • Manhattan *26*
- Maple & Almond Milkshake *180* • Margarita *54* • Martini *30* • Melon Medley *96*
- Melon Smoothie *106* • Mint Julep *22* • Moscow Mule *60* • Nectarine Melt *108*
- Old Fashioned *28* • Orange & Carrot Smoothie *172* • Orange & Lime Iced Tea *110*
- Pacific Smoothie *130* • Peach & Pineapple Smoothie *124* • Peppermint Ice *162*
- Peppermint Mocha *190* • Piña Colada *42* • Pineapple & Coconut Shake *122*
- Pineapple Crush *126* • Pineapple Soda *120* • Raspberry Cooler *144*
- Red Pepper Reactor *158* • Red Storm *174* • Rich Chocolate Shake *178*
- Rose Sunset *132* • Salty Dog *32* • Screwdriver *62* • Shirley Temple *94* • Sidecar *16*
- Singapore Sling *38* • Smooth Iced Coffee *186* • Spicy Banana Chill *114* • Stinger *18*
- Strawberry & Orange Smoothie *148* • Strawberry & Peach Smoothie *150*
- Summer & Citrus Fruit Punch *152* • Tequila Slammer *72* • Tequila Sunrise *56*
- Tom Collins *36* • Traditional Lemonade *136* • Vodga *80* • Watercress Float *170*
- What the Hell *84* • Whiskey Sour *24* • White Lady *34* • Wild Night Out *74*
- Zombie *50*